LUCKY YOU

Thoughts shared about Vidya's message . . .

"I am becoming a better person professionally and personally and trying to gain more and more knowledge with each passing day." — **S.A.**

"It helped me think differently about day-to-day activities, changing my mindset. Becoming more positive about things and not to compare myself with anyone but myself. Reflection and planning ahead are key to growth. I need to enjoy victories no matter how small." — **J.R.**

"Takeaways I will implement [are] not to procrastinate, focus on moments of joy, and try to do new and different things to change up routine." — **J.G.**

". . . continue my reflection exercise daily and use what I have learned to stretch myself as I am building my To-Do list for tomorrow." — **A.S.**

"The perspective gained was invaluable. I will be blocking off my calendar for time to reflect and plan, taking action now, not waiting for tomorrow or later. I will pay more attention while making decisions, realizing that each time there is a tradeoff." — **P.W.**

"I will start celebrating small victories, create more beneficial habits, plan better, and build an environment conducive for growth." — **D.O.**

"I've put some actions in place like checking in with myself and setting aside time for reflection, meditation, and self-care." — **T.K.**

"Intentional actions and decisions – I am working on planning more and reacting less. Consistency – I am taking daily positive actions and working toward turning those into habits." — **A.L.**

"The one thing I am going to implement is to consciously strive to be intentional so I can gain control of my day. This was a wake-up call. I have been wasting all my free time and was oblivious to it. I feel like I have my eyes opened." — **H.B**

"This was a great reminder that nothing worth doing is easy, but it starts with shifting the mindset. I am going to continue my journaling. I have a prompt where I write something I am grateful for every day and a positive thing that happened that day. I believe continuing this habit will help me stay on track with my growth even during days when it seems easier to give up." — **N.R.**

Thoughts shared about Vidya's message

LUCKY YOU

An Insider's Guide to Achieving Success and Finding Fulfillment in the Corporate World

VIDYA RAMAN

Lucky You
Copyright © 2023 Vidya Raman

All rights reserved. No part of this publication may be reproduced, distributed, or transmitted in any form or by any means, including photocopying, recording, or other electronic or mechanical methods, without the prior written permission of the publisher, except in the case of brief quotations embodied in critical reviews and certain other noncommercial uses permitted by copyright law. Permission requests should be sent to info@writewaypublishing.com. The links provided in this book were active at the time of publication, but may not remain so.

Printed in the United States of America
ISBN 978-1-956543-28-5

Book Design by CSinclaire Write-Design LLC
Cover by 100 Covers

This book is dedicated to my friends, coworkers, bosses, business partners, and detractors in the corporate world. You contributed to my experiences, learning, growth, and acquisition of wisdom. You paved the way to the present moment and, for that, I am truly grateful.

This book is also dedicated to YOU, for believing in yourself. You are a change agent, and you are on your way to unveiling your brilliance. I'm honored to be a part of your journey.

TABLE OF CONTENTS

Introduction 1

Chapter 1: PROJECT YOU 9

Chapter 2: THE FRAMEWORK 14

Chapter 3: SET THE STAGE FOR SUCCESS 18

Chapter 4: HARNESS HIDDEN GEMS 47

Chapter 5: IGNITE YOUR POWER................ 73

Chapter 6: FORGE YOUR PATH TO FULFILLMENT ... 94

Chapter 7: THRIVE AND FLOURISH 119

Chapter 8: LUCKY YOU 130

APPENDIX................................. 137

INTRODUCTION

> *"I work hard and produce results; surely that will get me noticed and promoted in my office."*
>
> *"I don't have the power to influence the bosses and bring about change because I don't have a prestigious title."*
>
> *"I'm not getting ahead in this company because talent and competency are not valued here and you know me, I am terrible at playing politics."*

If you believe any of these statements, this book is for you! In these pages, you will discover—just as I did—how to prove all these statements are wrong.

When you know you are competent and have a lot to offer at work, it can feel deeply frustrating when you are stuck in a role that does not challenge you. If you're naturally an overachiever, finding yourself in an underachieving situation can be a tough pill to swallow. It can be confusing and disheartening to be in a position where you feel like you're just taking orders, instead of leading with your skills and experience. You are bewildered by the career advancement of your peers and wonder when you will be picked for promotion. You sincerely want to make a difference in your organization.

If you're in this situation, you're not alone. Many people feel like they're not reaching their full potential at work, and it can be demoralizing.

I used to feel demoralized too. When I looked at my successful friends or read those notifications from LinkedIn about someone in my circle moving up the corporate ladder, I would feel a tinge of envy and then quickly conclude that some people were just lucky. Right place at the right time lucky.

What I am about to share with you in this book changed my life. There is a path to "lucky," and I'm going to walk you step-by-step along that path to help you architect and engineer your journey to feeling lucky, living your potential, and being fulfilled at work. It is my sincere hope that the framework, the steps, and the relatable and relevant examples in the pages ahead give you everything you need to achieve success and find fulfillment in the corporate world. I've walked this path myself as someone who was chronically underestimated and overlooked at work to finally finding my footing and becoming unstoppable. Here's my story. See if you relate.

For almost half of my corporate career, my potential was not recognized or respected. It wreaked havoc on me physically and mentally. I delivered high quality results, worked weekends, made personal sacrifices, and in return received "exceeds expectations" performance ratings year after year. But promotions remained out of my reach. So, I doubled down and did more, incorrectly assuming the quality of my work would finally melt the resistance.

There were times when I would share an idea in a meeting and wouldn't even get a nod of acknowledgment. I felt completely invisible. The lack of career advancement crushed my confidence and made me miserable. I knew something was wrong, but I had no idea what it was. Often, I would cry in the shower getting ready for work. Almost every Sunday evening a sense of dread would take over. I couldn't imagine surviving another full week at work. I thought about quitting many times, but concern for the well-being of my family stopped me in my tracks.

When I saw a less knowledgeable and less competent coworker, someone I had trained, get a promotion, it finally dawned on me that hard work and quality results were not the only defining criteria for career progression. Yes, I was a slow learner. I concluded that there was no one coming to rescue me. I had to rescue myself by taking ownership of my career.

Here's what I did. I chose my boss for that first "take ownership of my career" conversation. Armed with key points along with accompanying evidence carefully documented in my notepad, I marched into the meeting. Talk about being grossly underprepared for that important conversation! I did not know that I needed to work on my composure and demeanor as a part of my preparation. What my boss saw was comportment unbecoming of a professional.

With no emotional control in place, I jumped right into a directionless airing of grievances, interjected with sniffles and with tears raining down my cheeks. What I saw on the other side of the conference room table was an expressionless boss moving a box of tissues toward me. I blew my nose and realized that I had blown an important opportunity to gain an ally. My boss assured me that I was valued in the organization and encouraged me to keep doing what I was doing.

Naively, I somehow left the meeting with the hope that I would make the promotion list next year if I kept producing results. That did not happen.

With fear-based beliefs driving my decisions and actions, I allowed myself to languish in the same low-visibility role while college classmates moved into senior leadership. I became increasingly frustrated, questioned my personality and my accent, and even worried about the vibes I was giving off in everyday conversations. I figured I had blind spots I couldn't see but others could; however, no one was forthcoming about what was hindering my progress. To add insult to injury, my singular focus on deadlines and work quality caused me to miss clues that should have been obvious to me.

I recognized I was losing precious time with every birthday that rolled by. With no meaningful feedback at work, I turned to self-help books and CDs. They became the teachers I so desperately needed. Finally, I started to piece together a plan for growth. Just knowing that I was making a plan for progress was enough to lift me out of my misery.

My only desire at that time was to be recognized for my talents. To help with that goal, I cautiously and carefully harnessed what I had learned from my experiences and my self-help books to raise my visibility and profile at work. The promotions I coveted started to show up in quick succession. Throughout that time period, I continued to fine tune my career advancement strategies.

When I made it into the leadership ranks, I started to believe in myself and my approach. With that realization came a sense of haste to make up for all the time that had slipped away. I learned this type of growth is sometimes referred to as post-traumatic growth. It's the pain of unexpressed potential endured for years that provides the momentum for the career advancement that follows.

When I noticed opportunities in my chosen career track becoming scarce, my newfound confidence allowed me to craft a career move into an unfamiliar functional area. It paid off, and I thrived in my new leadership role. I took every opportunity to motivate and nurture my team, and they flourished. My diligence in applying insights from personal development and human motivation helped me become a wizard in identifying the motives of others, reading a room, and avoiding landmines. When some doors closed, I opened others. I had tools in my toolkit to craft a unique value proposition to succeed right where I was.

Given the faith in my capacity to inspire, I started coaching and mentoring others in the organization. I advocated for the high-potential but invisible employee. My own pain of not living my potential in my early career made me an empathetic and effective coach. I took on the role of a motivational coach for the employees in my organization who were lost and sought guidance from a direction perspective. I even started guiding managers who wanted to raise their team's engagement and performance. My mentees transformed right before my eyes and accelerated their careers forward. It was a source of great pride for me, and I basked in it.

After contributing more than twenty-five years to Corporate America and being the beneficiary of a steady paycheck and the accompanying financial security, I quit my well-compensated senior leadership role in 2022 to become a full-time corporate speaker and leadership coach.

At that time, companies were reeling from the consequences of the Great Resignation and quiet quitting trends. To address this expensive problem, some companies started instituting new protocols like fewer meetings to avoid employee burnout, new solutions to create opportunities for meaningful work, and increased spending on manager training. These top-down solutions are essential, but their impact is dependent on the quality of leadership at all levels of the organization.

I chose to address this problem by focusing on the individual employee, leaders included, and arming them with insights and tools to carve out a solution that meets them right where they are in their career. Every empowered employee then goes on to become a champion for a healthy corporate culture.

Having immersed myself in the good, bad, and ugly of the

corporate world for more than twenty-five years, I can relate to the frustration of unexpressed and unfulfilled potential. I not only experienced this pain but I heard about the same experiences from my coworkers, mentees, and clients. I have also witnessed many incredible career shifts, with some occurring in as little as a year. The best part is these employees did not have to move to another company. Success found them because they chose to singularly focus and commit to their success and fulfillment journey. They rescued themselves!

What does this mean for you? If you are feeling stuck in your corporate career, you may have resonated with some part of my story. You know that you are capable of so much more but you may not be sure where to begin making a change. After years of refining my professional transformation process and witnessing successful outcomes of my coworkers, I can confidently point you to the step-by-step approach contained in this book. It will help you craft your very own success and fulfillment journey starting right where you are.

CHAPTER 1

PROJECT YOU

You are likely reading this book because you have arrived at a point where accepting the status quo is getting more difficult by the day. Daily frustrations and annoyances are taking a toll on the quality of your life. You are regretting the wasted time. Maybe, like me, you have assumed if you continue to put in the effort and produce results consistently, your boss will eventually notice you and assign you high-visibility opportunities. Maybe, subconsciously, you have been afraid that if you were successful, your peers might like you less and you might lose your social network. There are plenty of excuses to go around to explain your current circumstance, some outside your control and some within.

Bosses, supervisors, managers, team leaders—most of you have them in your work life. What I am going to say next is not to excuse a "bad" boss you personally know. It is more a broad observation from my long corporate career. In general, bosses, supervisors, managers, and leaders are trying their best to deliver their own value, but sometimes their best falls short of the expectations held by those they manage.

Most employees want to be treated fairly and with respect, but the pressure cooker atmosphere within organizations often makes it difficult for managers to meet their people where they are. They have their own bosses to please and their own responsibilities to fulfill, which leaves them very little time to establish deep bonds with their direct reports. Besides that, they are not equipped or trained to be coaches and nurturers.

The premise of the framework of this book is to relax the bond of dependency with your boss and, instead, make you the driver of your career progress. You will take control over your own career trajectory and job satisfaction by digging deep into your own personal power and using it to help influence change. And you'll do this by growing your awareness and by executing simple daily rituals. It's surprising how the world around you transforms when you transform yourself.

This book is designed to help you achieve career progression and job satisfaction through this personal transformation. No doubt you have heard this same claim more than once, but don't quit reading. This approach *will* help you. The plan you will construct for your personal transformation will be uniquely yours, while the foundation this approach will give you, that layer that provides a level surface with a good load-bearing capacity, will prove its strength and resilience over and over again. It's not visible on the surface, but it is necessary and instrumental in helping you not only carry the weight of your daily responsibilities and challenges but to open you up to new possibilities and vistas you wouldn't have considered previously.

Here's the premise we're working with: You know you have value to offer your employer, but for the leaders in your company to recognize your potential, they first need to know you. You may have heard that people do business with people they know, like, and trust. You can influence outcomes at work when people know, like, and trust you.

Often, what limits someone's career progress is the "know" you part. Managing your exposure and visibility in the company is an acquired skill and can be nurtured with the insights laid out in this book. Being underestimated is crushing your spirit and creating mounting frustration. You are not feeling successful—or as successful as you should. Here's an important thought: Philosophers, both ancient and modern, attribute failure in life not to the lack of material success but rather to the lack of living up to your potential.

You're not alone in your experiences or your feelings. Both the Great Resignation and quiet quitting trends point to individuals stepping away physically or mentally in so many workplaces. You can be an agent of positive change in the face of this. You can be the one who takes positive action for yourself, and the benefit is then experienced by your employer as well.

What will this transformation known as PROJECT YOU entail? You'll be growing your awareness, setting a few goals, stepping out of your comfort zone occasionally, marking milestones, finding your bona fide place, and prioritizing your time instead of allowing your time to be managed for you. This journey to fulfillment will not be taxing but, instead, will reduce stress by awakening your spirit to the pleasures of the day.

Joyful Expectations on Your Journey

1. Working toward achievable goals and celebrating each success will bring you joy.

2. Building better connections at work will let you be yourself and lift your spirits.

3. Silencing unfounded fears and stepping out of your comfort zone will boost your confidence.

4. Discovering new insights will flood you with unconventional solutions to old problems.

5. Owning and managing your time will buy you space in your day for regular breaks.

6. Having time to breathe deeply and center yourself will keep you in control of your agenda.

7. Embracing gratitude as a daily practice will fuel your tank with joy.

Maybe you like what you've read so far, but you aren't sure if the time is right for you to begin your own transformation. You're juggling work, family responsibilities, and who knows what else. The thought of adding one more task to your daily agenda seems overwhelming. You're not sure you have the bandwidth to do one more thing.

If these thoughts are rumbling in your mind, ask yourself this: What is more important than taking care of yourself to sustain a life and a career that are meaningful and fulfilling? What is more pressing than PROJECT YOU? Your personal growth is what helps you show up the way you want to be seen by others—bosses, coworkers, family, and friends. Onward and Upward. Let's kick off PROJECT YOU!

CHAPTER 2

THE FRAMEWORK

The choices you make every day shape your destiny. Who you are influences your choices. Once you decipher what propels you forward, recognize what holds you back, and understand what sabotages your best laid plans, you can start becoming the person you want to be. The question is, how do you decipher those components?

Most executive coaches will direct their senior executive clients toward a self-awareness deep dive. You need to know yourself, have confidence in your abilities, be comfortable in your own skin, and have a vision for yourself first before exerting your influence and authority on others. When leaders operate without a sense of self and purpose, they lose their credibility and their capacity to influence. That importance of understanding self and purpose is true for all of us, not just senior executives.

Organizational initiatives and projects typically solve a

big problem with high stakes and have a defined desired outcome. Often, projects are complex and lead project participants into unfamiliar territories. The best outcomes line up with expectations and desires when plans are set and executed consistently, thoughtfully, and intentionally. These same things will hold true for your personal transformation project, the most important project you will ever manage!

PROJECT YOU is designed to help you craft your own success and fulfillment plan. No permission is needed. You will feel empowered to drive your transformation within the boundaries of your current role at work. Let me show you how to do this.

Introducing S.H.I.F.T.

There are five steps in the S.H.I.F.T. framework:

1. Set the stage for success
2. Harness hidden gems
3. Ignite your power
4. Forge your path to fulfillment
5. Thrive and flourish

Before you get started on this transformational PROJECT YOU, take time to identify and recognize where you are now in your inner world. This is just for you. Capture your thoughts in a notebook, so you can come back to them later when prompted. (But not until then!) Or maybe you prefer to digitally record your thoughts by voice or video. Use the method that works best for you to capture information during your journey, starting with this "before" snapshot.

Here are some thoughts to gather for your snapshot:

- Do you feel seen at work?

- Do you feel valued?

- Are you appreciated?

- Are you and your work deployed well?

- Who are your allies?

- Who would you like to be your ally?

- What are your perceived (by you) failures?

- What causes you the most frustration?

- What creates the most pain or angst in you?

- What do you see as your strengths?

- What do you want to change about yourself?

- One a scale of 1 to 10 with 10 being the highest, what is your job satisfaction level?

Now that you have your BEFORE snapshot, you are ready to start to S.H.I.F.T.!

The next chapter is the first step of the S.H.I.F.T. framework, and it is the longest one in this book. It's a foundational step very much like the prep phase of a room painting project. The outcome of painting a room is dependent on preparations that take time and patience. You need to remove furniture and wall art, take down window treatments, repair holes and cracks, maybe sand the walls and then clean thoroughly, and protect the floors and trim before you begin painting. Without the right foundational prep, the painting outcome will not have the high-quality results you desire. Step one in the S.H.I.F.T. framework is Set the Stage for Success. This begins the preparation that guarantees your desired outcome for PROJECT YOU. Take your time with it.

CHAPTER 3

SET THE STAGE FOR SUCCESS

Did my story of invisibility at work and seeing others around me promoted (but not me) resonate with you? I'll never forget the deep embarrassment and shame I experienced when a new employee who was curious to learn the lay of the land asked me out to lunch. At lunch, she asked me about my tenure and my title at work. I hesitated and then almost whispered the response, and she said, "Wow, only that after a decade of work here."

She may have been untactful, but she was right. For people who did not know my talents, competency, and skills, I appeared not to care about career advancement. But I did care. I was already stewing about my predicament, and this honest observation shook me up and caused me to enter a period of passive-aggressive retaliation at work. However, with my ambitious, driven, and go-getter spirit, the checked-out phase did not last long.

Here's something important to realize. *Nobody was suffering as much as I was from my situation. No one is suffering as much as you are from your situation.* Accepting the status quo is essentially a slap in the face of your dreams and aspirations. When you are unable to express your potential, then pain, dissatisfaction, and self-diminishing thoughts build inside of you. They stay with you. Does this sound familiar? Is your unexpressed potential causing you deep pain?

The S.H.I.F.T. framework being shared with you to help you grow professionally took years to craft and refine. It has been tested, successfully, start to finish, first on myself and then on my mentees and clients, individually and in corporate group settings. It works.

You are still reading this book because you know you deserve better. You want to stop feeling underestimated, unappreciated, and underutilized at work. You crave visibility and exposure in your organization. You understand you have to rescue yourself. You are ready to S.H.I.F.T. and transform.

The good news is the S.H.I.F.T. approach is logical and very doable to create a desired transformation. The aptitude, skills, and power you need to bring about the change you want are already within you. You just need to wake them up and nurture them. Are you ready to start?

Make a Commitment

- Know that your future self is worth your time and energy.

- Plan for dedicated time to work on your growth plan.

- Have a work calendar or a personal calendar for quick flags, reminders, and more to serve as an easy and quick tracker of your consistent effort and progress.

- Have a person in mind to serve as an accountability partner.

- Have a few people in mind to call on periodically as a sounding board or a feedback source.

- Use a notebook or a folder on your laptop to record notes, observations, and comments during your transformation.

Start with Preparation

You know planning and preparation are essential to the success of a project, and PROJECT YOU is no exception. Do the work. Take the needed amount of time. Don't skip steps and don't shortcut. Based on your experience and where you are in your career, some parts of the plan will move more quickly than others. That is to be expected.

If you create the stage setting and it is grand, everyone who enters will play their part. — **Morris Lapidus**

Reading this quote from the view of personal and professional growth, the more effort you make in understanding who you are and how you work with others (your stage), the more others will engage with you and assist your climb to success. The first step of this transformation, then, is set the stage for success. This is a critical preparation step. This is what draws the attention of others. Just as Morris Lapidus tells us, the richer, more vibrant, and grander the stage setting, the more magnetic the appeal will be. You will be using the tools of *self-awareness* and *social awareness* to build your stage, your foundation. First comes self-awareness.

Self-Awareness — Know Yourself

What is this thing called self-awareness? It's the ability to see yourself clearly. To understand who you are, how others see you, and how you fit into the world. It gives you insights into what you hold dear, what upsets you, what triggers you, and what drives your daily choices. Self-awareness gives you understanding, power, and a sense of direction.

Growing your self-awareness will give you a deeper understanding of what success looks like to you. You will have better and healthier conversations and that leads to better relationships. You'll find yourself more creative and more confident. According to Travis Bradberry and Jean Greaves, authors of *Emotional Intelligence 2.0*, eighty-three percent of people with high self-awareness are top performers, while only 2 percent of bottom performers display this trait. It should not be lost on you that self-aware people perform better at work and are considered promotion worthy. This is what you are striving to achieve.

Your Current Awareness Level

In your notebook write your responses to the three questions below. This is just free-flow writing to describe what you know about yourself. This is a warm-up. You will refine this as you grow. You may not always like what you see in these answers, but that will help you know what you want to change.

1. What are your strengths?

2. What are your weaknesses?

3. What do you enjoy at work?

Your answers will bring into sharper focus your current awareness level. The next time you chat with a spouse or a close friend, ask them about their perceptions of you. Lead with the first two questions if they fit. Listen carefully and uncritically. This is important. Compare their opinions to your own. It's fine to share your own thoughts with them.

In your notebook, capture your observations on any disconnect between your thoughts and what others perceive. Their insights may surprise you, and some may be real eye-openers.

Going Deeper

Next, take a deeper look into self-awareness. This time you will be considering five topics: your values, interests, strengths, temperament, and activity peak periods. You may be tempted to rush through this exercise, but please resist that temptation. Remember, you are building the *stage* to showcase your future self. Do not compromise the foundation that is meant to support you. During your transformation, you should revisit your stage periodically for regular maintenance and enhancements. Circumstances will change. You will change. Keeping your notebook updated with continued revelations about yourself will prove to be very beneficial.

VALUES

You've likely read or heard about companies and organizations sharing their "core values" with employees and customers. Maybe you even know your own company's core values. But your task now is to get clear on *your* core values that guide *your* decisions. Taking time to reflect on what values are most important to you will help you in setting your stage.

Writing about values may feel vague and ambiguous. Let's start with a basic definition. Values are opinions that you deem important. They influence your choices and the way you live every day. They are beliefs that are significant to you personally and help define who you are as an individual. Values play an important role in how you set goals, respond to situations, and make decisions. Values determine your priorities, and, deep down, they're probably the measures you use, knowingly or unknowingly, to tell if your life is turning out the way you intended.

When the things that you do and the way you behave align with your values, you feel satisfied and complete. When your outside actions are in accordance with your inside values, you will experience less inner conflict. Roy A. Disney said, "When your values are clear to you, making decisions becomes easier."

But when decisions don't match your personal values, you feel unhappy and out of alignment. If your core value is integrity, and you operate "out of alignment" with this value by playing dirty politics like the office bullies do, those actions will create disharmony in your spirit and leave you feeling broken.

There are many amazing sites dedicated to personal values that guide you in identifying your core values, but you can do this work on your own. Think back to the best and worst moments in your life. Consider what these experiences reveal about your core values. For example, if you love sharing what you know, it's possible that teaching others is an important value for you. Conversely, if you value striving for excellence, you can get deeply dissatisfied in a role that does not challenge you. The values we admire are typically personified by people we respect. As you think about the values that drive you, in your notebook write down the names of five people you admire and the values that they embody.

Take this consideration of values you hold now to another

level. Who is your future self going to be? What personality traits, attributes, and characteristics would your future self exhibit? How do these compare with how you see yourself today? Based on this comparison, what decisions do you need to make to build your future self? Make these lists in your notebook. Begin right now making the necessary decisions and embodying those desired traits in your daily choices.

While values are mostly stable, they can take on greater or lesser importance as you change and grow. Keeping in touch with your values is a lifelong exercise. Take time to periodically assess your value priorities. Let your values stretch and grow with you. Here's a sampling of commonly held values: Honesty, Kindness, Courage, Excellence, Loyalty, Humility, Leadership, Integrity, Empathy, Recognition, Generosity, Selflessness, Sustainability, Altruism, Family, Flexibility, and Tolerance.

Remember, you are on a journey to take charge of your career. The very nature of the journey is making changes in yourself to become more visible, to shine on the stage you set. Where you are now is not where you will be as the journey progresses—if you do the work.

Here's something I did that you may want to consider doing. Before every major career shift in my life, I took an online personal values assessment. Doing this let me see where I had changed and determine if any of my values (or their priority) had shifted. This assessment helped me immensely when I decided to move from a technical role to a business role and when I finally decided to become a speaker and coach. For a small investment in time and money, an assessment can help you begin to uncover the real priorities in your life. The results can get you thinking more clearly.

Online Values Assessments

There are many free or low-cost online values assessment websites that can help you. You can do your own research in this area. The assessments are relatively short, so do not take much time to complete. Just search "free personal values assessment" or "personal values assessment." The one I used was *htttps://www.valuescentre.com/tools-assessments/pva/*. I have shared a PDF of a portion of my values assessment from 2020 in the Appendix.

You may be tempted to skip this task of assessing your values because it feels like work. If you skip this step to move on to the next, it will be analogous to starting a long journey without your GPS. You may arrive somewhere you don't want to be. Do the work.

If you have not already done so:

- Capture at least five core values you hold now.

- List the values you see in five people you admire.

- Identify the values you want for your future self.

Take the time to describe your values and write about scenarios where your values (your compass or GPS) will direct you.

This will help you more easily and naturally incorporate them in your life. Once you feel relatively confident that you have a good sense of your current values and the values you aspire to, you will be ready to move on to examining your interests.

INTERESTS

A good approach to uncovering your interests is to look in the rearview mirror of your life. Think of when you felt energized and completely focused. Think about the times when you were the happiest and most fulfilled. Find examples from both your career and personal life. This will ensure some balance in your answers. Engaging in a hobby might make this list. Think about those moments that filled you with enthusiasm: What were you doing? Were you with other people? Who were they? What other factors contributed to this energized state? Record all this in your notebook.

Now do the opposite. Think about the times that did not create positive feelings and the tasks that you dread doing. Are there certain responsibilities that create an instant desire to procrastinate? Record this information in your notebook.

Can you see where this is going? If you want to be very intentional in collecting this data, try tracking two weeks of activity on your calendar app. Identify and flag activities that energize you and those that drain you. Keep a running list of each. In addition to increasing self-awareness, this exercise has two more potential rewards, one in the present and one in the future. For now, you can improve the quality of your days by being intentional about doing more of what energizes you. And for the future, you may well find you are recapturing productive time from working less on draining tasks and more on those that fulfill you.

You may be wondering how that is even possible without compromising your productivity at work. It's an incremental approach, and as you process the other sections in this framework, this will feel easier. The immediate goal here with considering interests is to increase the joy you receive from daily activities, not to completely revamp your daily calendar to include only your passions.

Like a prior client of mine, some of you may discover that researching market data and digging deep into the numbers is what excites you. Other interests you may uncover are data visualization, content summarization, developing awe-inspiring presentations, delivering presentations, preparing financial statements, and more.

When I maintained an activity log for just two weeks at work, I discovered that I felt depleted on days when I had to spend long hours documenting project details. That was a tough revelation, because I was a project manager and regular documentation was a requirement. In time, I managed to reduce the time I spent on that one activity that drained me. I automated some of it and delegated another chunk to a colleague who loved documenting and organizing. I was left with a smaller segment of the task that depleted me.

If you don't work on your own energized versus drained log,

you may miss the option to strategize and improve the quality of your day as you walk or sprint toward your goal.

When you have clarity on your interests, move on to strengths.

STRENGTHS

To gain a more focused understanding of your strengths and weaknesses, take at least thirty minutes and review the lists of your strengths and weaknesses that you made when you began this self-awareness section. First, take some time to reflect on your strengths. Having completed the exercise on interests, this should move quickly. Based on the self-awareness work you have done so far, would anything on this list change? This is the identification of your core competencies as you see them. Here is a key distinction between interests and competency: you may have an interest but may not necessarily be good at it, and you may have a core competency or strength but not necessarily enjoy doing it.

Everyone has something of value to offer others. Some know what it is, and some are yet to discover it. Discovery is easier if you are present and paying attention to the clues around you. Here's an interesting fact. Those around you likely recognize strengths that you don't notice in yourself, often because they are things that come easily and naturally to you. What skills or traits do other people associate with you? Ask your boss, colleagues, and associates. Do you receive compliments for a particular talent or skill? Add these things to your strengths list.

When you review your lists with your strengths and interests (from earlier in this chapter), you may not find harmony and cohesiveness between them. That is fairly common. Filling your days with opportunities that showcase your strengths and participating in things that interest you have the potential to put a spring in your step. If you do find a match between a strength and an interest, you may have stumbled upon a passion to explore further.

Engaging in activities that match your strengths is essential to confidence building. Knowing these particular strengths and developing them to a mastery level is how you raise your profile and relevance in the organization. This is your potential calling card for career advancement. Recognizing and honing your strengths will help channel your attention and your time into the right activities.

As you are adding your strengths on the list, remember you don't need to have a long list. In fact, if you've included more than seven items, you're probably starting to focus too much on strengths that aren't that significant or are not in full alignment with your interests.

Now on to your weaknesses. You can use these questions to guide your thoughts as you consider your weakness list:

- What have others had to help you with on more than one occasion?

- What areas were identified by your boss during your last performance evaluation?

- What tasks or responsibilities cause you the most frustration or discomfort in your work?

- What skills do you admire and see in others that you would like more of?

After you have your list of strengths and weaknesses from your perspective, it's time to get input from those closest to you: a significant other, your mentor, peers, and close friends. You may discover strengths you had not previously recognized and become aware of weaknesses that may be hindering your career progress.

You may have discovered that you are highly competent with data analytics, project organization, presentation decks, or documentation. You may also have uncovered that you are a gifted conversationalist, a people magnet, a problem solver, or a consensus builder. Did any of these essential career advancement skills show up when talking to your peers, mentor, or boss: communication, leadership, confidence, working relationships, or a proactive way of working?

Knowing what traits or skills people recognize in you will give you guidance and direction to enhance your personal brand. If you are detail-oriented, know that strength and use it to your advantage. As a project leader, I loved working with team members who were precise and paid attention to detail. If you discovered that you are good with people, it is likely that you are a good listener, helpful, and empathetic. This strength can help you excel when managing people.

Consider your list of weaknesses. Did your own assessment and that of your close contacts align? How do these weaknesses impact your work? What can you do to minimize their effect, especially if they play an essential role in your work? Are there courses you can take to increase knowledge or improve skills? Could a coach guide your transformation in a particular area? What daily practice can you add to your routine to overcome the weakness? For example, going to bed earlier to be better rested for work or getting to work fifteen minutes earlier for a little quiet time to organize your day. Or if better communication skills are what you seek, could you join a local Toastmasters club, an organization dedicated to the craft of communication and leadership? I have seen many transformations, including my own, through actively engaging in Toastmasters club meetings.

Capture a few observations and thoughts in your notebook about what you have discovered about yourself and what this means for you. If you are still not entirely clear on your strengths and weaknesses from your own and your colleagues' assessments or if you would like to go deeper, consider completing a personality assessment. This is not necessary, but they can be interesting and perhaps instructive. Here are three well-known indicators that your company's learning resources may offer plus a free option:

- **The Myers Briggs Type Indicator** (MBTI) is popular as a corporate-level personality assessment. It measures you within a framework of four areas: energy (introvert versus extravert/also spelled extrovert), decision-making, taking in information, and approaching the outside world. There are free versions of this test called Jung Personality Test.

- The **DISC** method. DISC is an acronym that stands for the four main personality profiles described in the DISC model: (D)ominance, (I)nfluence, (S)teadiness, and (C)onscientiousness. **D personalities** tend to be confident and place an emphasis on accomplishing bottom-line results. **I personalities** tend to be more open and place an emphasis on relationships and influencing or persuading others. **S personalities** tend to be dependable and place their emphasis on cooperation and sincerity. **C personalities** tend to place the emphasis on quality, accuracy, expertise, and competency.

- The **StrengthsFinder** assessment determines your top five "Talent Themes" with terms like Achiever, Learner, and Relator as well as terms like Restorative, Strategic, and Maximizer.

- If getting a paid personality test in your company is not a viable option, there is a free **Big Five Personality Test** available online.

Channeling your efforts in the right areas needs careful consideration based on the findings in this step. Blindly focusing solely on areas your peers and supervisors call out may take you to a destination you may regret later. You want to shine in a way that differentiates you, but also that aligns with your core values and interests to give you the satisfaction you want to feel in your daily routines. Always remember that you are building your unique selling proposition. Being just like everyone does not merit the promotion and advancement you seek.

Once you have considered your lists and have spent some time reflecting on how you are going to leverage your strengths and address your weaknesses, you are ready to move forward to temperament.

TEMPERAMENT

Knowing and understanding your temperament intimately will make your career and life journey a lot easier to navigate and will make challenges feel less intimidating. In psychology, temperament broadly refers to consistent behavior that is biologically based and is relatively independent of learning, values, and attitudes. In essence, temperament describes your inborn preferences. Here are a few questions for you to ponder. First, think about and answer them in terms of your work life. Then go through the list again and answer based on your personal life—your natural inclination. Write your answers in your notebook.

1. Are you energized by quiet moments of solitude or by being with others?

2. Are you a planner or do you prefer spontaneity?

3. Do you listen more or talk more?

4. Do you make decisions based on feelings or facts?

5. Do you prefer details, or do you prefer to focus on the big picture?

6. During idea generation, are you deeply rooted in the reality of constraints or are you a blue-sky visionary?

7. Are you at your productive best right before an approaching deadline or is your high productivity not influenced by a deadline?

Some of your answers may have changed when you consider personal preferences instead of your job responsibilities. For example, at work you may be required to plan execution steps in precise detail, but your natural preference in your personal life may be to go with the flow and be spontaneous. As humans, we shift our behavior to match the situation.

Knowing the answers to these questions will make you aware of your natural inclinations and allow you to govern them accordingly. For example, a senior leader I used to work with was an introvert, and he enjoyed his quiet moments of solitude. Those moments fueled and energized him. However, given his role, he acclimated himself to becoming comfortable in large groups and to standing in front of the large audiences giving his quarterly presentations. After a day or two of heavy social interactions, he retreated to his safe space of solitude to recharge his batteries.

Recognizing your natural preference in answering any of

these questions does not mean you cannot shift toward the opposite end of or anywhere along the spectrum. Early in my leadership role, I was invested in "facts" and all the constraints they placed on us as we ideated on new corporate initiatives. I operated within the boundaries of a box. During that phase, I partnered with a new leader who was on the opposite side of the spectrum, a BlueSky creative.

As a big picture person, he came up with ideas that in my opinion were not grounded in reality. I recall my sheer frustration in working with ideas that would never find a corporate sponsor to get off the ground. Only later in my career did I see value in that type of visionary thinking. Over time I opened myself to think in terms of ideal solutions without constantly limiting myself with known constraints. This shift in thinking helped my career advance and let me find roles that enhanced my meaning and fulfillment score. The fact that I am a realist did not change.

Of course, going against the grain of your natural preferences can make any task complex, frustrating, and draining. Continuously fighting against your natural tendencies can make you moody and less agreeable to others. No one who is on a growth plan wants to come across as disagreeable. By recognizing what your natural tendencies are, you can find ways to mitigate any frustration and reduce discomfort.

Write in your notebook about possible ways your natural temperament could guide your actions. For example, a mentee of mine was at her productive best right before a deadline. Without a deadline, she would feel a little lost and unfocused. When she worked on projects that had not been assigned deadlines, she manufactured deadlines for subtasks and placed them on her calendar. This approach aligned well with her natural preference for a looming deadline.

When you are ready, move on to activity peak periods.

ACTIVITY PEAK PERIODS

This category refers to *when* you like to do things. It has to do with your biorhythm, often referred to as your circadian rhythm. Yes, this is another category that is based on your natural inclinations. As you would expect, working in your peak-energy times can elevate your efficiency, productivity, and performance. Here are two questions to consider:

- Do you identify as a morning person or a night owl?

- What time (or times) of the day is (are) most productive for you?

When you schedule activities for the time in the day when you are at your best, you are respecting your innate biology. Whatever your natural disposition, your best work and throughput are produced when you are in alignment with your natural biorhythm. Maximizing the times when your energy is the highest will make you feel like you are winning the day.

Pay attention to what your body is telling you and schedule your most important work for that period of the day. The easy and less important work can be fitted in for your off-peak times, but essential growth-dedicated activities should align with your natural rhythm. I have known my natural rhythm from the time I was a teenager. I wake up between four and five o'clock every morning. I dedicate the early hours to my most important priorities of the day. During my long tenure in the corporate arena, I had most of my critical tasks completed by nine o'clock. I also know many highly productive and creative night owls.

Once you have captured a comment or two in your notebook about making the most of your peak periods, give yourself a round of applause. This self-awareness step was a heavy lift. You deeply evaluated and considered how **v**alues, **i**nterests, **s**trengths, **t**emperament, and **a**ctivity times play into who you are. You have brought into focus the VISTA that is uniquely you through the lens of self-awareness.

You're now ready to move to the second tool in Set the Stage for Success: social awareness.

Social Awareness

This step needs your observation prowess to be in top form. You need to stay present and alert during key moments of your work day. Don't ignore those casual conversations with colleagues. You will be conducting a study, incognito of course, of the people in your environment. You will need some time for reflection and some notebook updates. Your research and refinement effort could carry on for a while with new insights bubbling up periodically. You will get better at understanding and working with others as time goes on. You do not have to complete a defined amount of research for this study to proceed with your transformation, but it is important that you grasp the concepts discussed and continue your observations.

WATCH YOURSELF

Watch yourself in action. It may seem odd at first, but you will get good at this with time. Nonverbal signals in your daily conversations carry more impact than your words. People trust your nonverbal signals more than your words. It's essential to think about your facial expressions, your tone of voice, your body language, and your hand gestures. Observe other people's reactions to you. Do their reactions seem positive, neutral, or negative?

Are you presenting to others as approachable, polite, and likable? Is your expression open? Is your tone of voice appropriate? Do you see smiles and head nods when you speak to a person? Do they exhibit positive and open body language to you? If not, what do you see?

Have you ever been asked why are you upset or why are you angry when you did not feel that emotion? This kind of question may be coming from your facial expressions, body language, or tone of voice. Do people look away from you as soon as you start talking? Are you being too abrupt? Do they fail to meet your eyes? Do your coworkers respond to you with curt answers? Why? Are they simply rushed and overwhelmed, or is it something else? Look for patterns of reactions to you and compare those reactions to the reactions received by a coworker or well-respected supervisor. What is the same and what is different about those interactions? What is your takeaway on these observations?

EXPRESSING WARMTH

A simple gesture of greeting people by name and genuinely complimenting them or asking a friendly question can work wonders when it comes to building relationships. Managers who express warmth are more approachable and get ranked higher in evaluations. Rarely does anyone approach an emotionally withdrawn manager with a genuine problem.

W.I.I.F.M

The acronym W.I.I.F.M. (What's in it for me?) is not just for sales and marketing pitches. It's a powerful tool for building connections at work. Strive to enter any conversation knowing the needs of the other party. Leaders who have learned the art of connection are able to effectively communicate ideas, establish buy-in, and attract followers. People who connect with others have better relationships, experience less conflict, and get more things done than those who do not put in the effort to build connections. When you truly connect with others—one-on-one or in groups—a sense of community is created. By creating a community that respects you and enjoys working with you, your capacity to influence grows.

ACTIVE LISTENING

One of the most effective social skills you can develop is active listening. Active listening is a show of respect. It will serve you well. Active listening is an action verb. It is giving the other party your undivided attention. It is not about a clever comeback or response but more about what is being said and not said. With time you will get very good at "listening" between the lines. Everyone wants to be heard. Always have your empathy hat on and be humble.

The other way active listening works to your benefit is by reading the nonverbal cues of the person. People, especially at work, wear masks to hide their true feelings. But often they unknowingly offer you clues through their body language. An inability to make direct eye contact can indicate boredom, disinterest, or even deceit—especially when someone looks away. If they stand close to you and start mirroring your actions, it could indicate that they are trying to build a connection with you. Dig a little deeper into this topic to get good at it.

RELATIONSHIPS

Often we are busy at work and rush through our interactions. Our focus is on results and not the people. We call someone when we need something. That is a transactional relationship. Where possible, schedule time in your week to build meaningful productive relationships. A cultivated relationship will increase your odds of getting prompt responses to your requests. Your climb up the corporate ladder needs these relationships because they have the power to champion your climb directly or indirectly.

GOOD INTENT

In work environments, it is important to understand that different teams have different priorities and motives. Often you may find yourself at cross purposes with another team in the same company. The sales team may be at odds with the risk management team, for example, or the marketing team with the product team. Often, individuals see reality very differently. That is why assuming "subjective" realities in your daily interaction will lead to less conflict.

Individual realities are shaped by upbringing, belief systems, and current circumstances. Assuming that subjective realities exist helps set expectations at the right levels and leads to more open and honest conversations. It enables us to walk in other people's shoes. Nothing ruins a good mood opportunity like an ongoing conflict. A mantra I have shared with others to lessen time wasted on ongoing conflicts is "always assume good intent" in others' actions and reactions. Yes, it is hard to do that in certain situations.

When it gets extremely difficult to assume good intentions in certain situations, you may want to confirm your suspicions.

Especially in terms of the resistance you are experiencing. You may suspect that there is resistance, but you are not absolutely certain. In such situations, consider the option of *trial balloons*. It could be a crafty conversation setup or a clever and well-considered email to gauge the temperature. The intention here is not to trick the other party but to confirm your suspicion of resistance and help you move on. If a door has been closed, why keep knocking at it?

ATTITUDE OF SERVICE

Adopting an attitude of service will help you find meaning in your daily life. Seek out opportunities to help others on your team or to serve a cause. This recommendation may seem counterintuitive when you feel you are getting no help from others. This one may take a lot out of you when your spirit is struggling, but the benefit will be sizable. This one is a win-win for all parties. Your self-worth will increase, and your leaders will notice your generous spirit.

LIKEABILITY

Likability is a double-edged sword at work. Wanting to be liked is universal. Nothing is wrong with that. To varying degrees, most of us seek the approval of others. Let's talk about how it can hurt us though. When someone takes on a people-pleaser identity, they start compromising their personal preferences in order to be liked. They abandon their "self," their feelings, and their true nature. They incorrectly assume that by being agreeable they will be seen as kind. They can't say no, they feel responsible for how others feel, and they apologize even when it is not their fault.

This behavior can backfire because it can be interpreted by others as being less confident and less competent. If career progression is a goal, watch out for behaviors that can be perceived as subservient. Don't play small just to be liked.

Moving on, there is a helpful side of likability. Building meaningful partnerships at work needs both likability and credibility. Be genuinely interested in others and listen actively. Follow up with someone just to chat and not because you need something from them. Your outreach will feel less transactional and more sincere. Your genuine interest in others will move up your likability score and possibly your career trajectory. Follow the Goldilocks principle when it comes to likability, not too hot and not too cold, not too hard and not too soft.

Early in my project management career, deadlines and results were all that mattered to me. I regularly reminded everyone on the project team about their upcoming deliverables and was relentless in my pursuit of hitting targets. This meant others had to move their priorities to accommodate my ask. I was always friendly, but my work relationships were mostly transactional. Once I gained a deeper understanding about relationships and human motivation, I pulled back on my hard-nosed approach and worked diligently at nurturing relationships. Much to my surprise, I discovered that empathy, generosity, and respect in everyday interactions lead to higher productivity and performance. Who knew that results could be achieved without a barrage of reminders and accountability meetings!

UNHELPFUL TRAITS

Some unhelpful traits people unconsciously exhibit may preclude them from forming meaningful connections. Here are some to be aware of:

- **Insecurity** – displayed in your words, body language, and actions
- **Bossiness** – forcing others to bend to your wishes
- **Defensiveness** – accepting no blame and shifting it onto others
- **Self-Centeredness** – focusing entirely on your success and talking incessantly about yourself
- **Ungratefulness** – never acknowledging the help of others
- **Impatience** – rushing to get to successful outcomes without considering the priorities of others

Likewise, people who present themselves frequently as victims or complainers generally find it hard to get traction in their professional growth.

After studying these social awareness insights, how do feel about what you have learned? Can you add some of your own insights to this list? How does information gained from social awareness help you better understand your bosses, leaders, coworkers, their realities, and their motives? Write down your thoughts in your notebook.

Mastering social awareness is a significant and ongoing effort. Spend some time reflecting on the material presented here. The energy and effort you put into relationships will pay the highest dividends in terms of your career trajectory.

When you feel you understand the insights in this important preparation chapter at a deeper level than when you started, your **stage** is on sound footing. You are ready to move forward in your S.H.I.F.T. journey and Harness Hidden Gems.

CHAPTER SUMMARY

- Studies have proven that self-aware people perform better at work and in life.

- Social awareness or social intelligence learned and developed not only supports career acceleration but also sets you up for overall fulfillment in life.

- The process of behavior change requires you to raise your self-awareness and social awareness and that takes a deep commitment, a dedicated amount of prep time, and keen observation skills for benchmarking your current awareness levels.

CHAPTER 4

HARNESS HIDDEN GEMS

Congratulations! You have taken a major leap forward. Clarity on self-awareness and social awareness is critical to your transformation journey. Savor this accomplishment to energize you for your final phase in foundation building—learning from your history. To continue with the wall painting analogy, you are in the final phase of prep before painting can begin.

> *Those who cannot remember the past are condemned to repeat it.* — **George Santayana**

As a corporate employee, you are familiar with the concept of lessons learned. Most companies initiate a post-implementation survey after a project is implemented. The goal of the survey is to receive feedback from stakeholders and project partners. Feedback is categorized and the resulting document is a snapshot of lessons learned. One of the objectives is to improve the area(s) flagged as "poor" in the survey.

In this step of PROJECT YOU, you will extract lessons learned from your past experiences and work history to crystallize and set up the next set of actions in your transformation journey. When you look back at your experiences and evaluate them, you will find priceless lessons or "hidden gems." The knowledge gained from closely and constructively examining your past experiences will give you a sense of confidence when you start your strategic march toward your goal. By harnessing the hidden gems you uncover, you will not be starting from scratch but from an advanced vantage point that will ensure you get your future self to your right destination faster. You are putting learning from your own experience to work for you.

> *Every experience, good or bad, is a priceless collector's item.* — **Isaac Marion**

Constructive feedback can be sorely lacking in corporate life. You may have asked your supervisor for feedback many times and after those sessions, you may have been left wanting. The responses often seem superficial with no specifics, making it hard to nail down your perceived weaknesses or to be clear about your strengths. More candid feedback would have provided the clarity of direction you were seeking. To be fair, it is no easy task for managers, even well-meaning managers, to give candid and constructive feedback, but this is a topic for a different book! For now, you are in the take-charge-of-your-career mode, so the work falls on you to scout out the lessons you've learned through your past work experiences. You will find what you uncover in the steps ahead illuminating if you do the work.

Focus on Hits and Misses in Your Work Experience

Here's your task. Leave room for three lists in your notebook. Let's start with two lists initially. One list is for highpoints where you or your team were acknowledged for work done or a problem solved, and the second list is for situations when you or your team did not accomplish the mission. Be ready to document your answers as candidly as possible as you read and evaluate questions presented below. Looking back at your answers is what makes the excavation of hidden gems possible. You may uncover that you showed your frustrations openly and often in a prior project for example. Even if you were justified in your actions, complaining and sharing your frustration openly causes others to perceive you as a complainer and not a problem-solver.

Let's move on to the questions. Review previous work initiatives, one by one, that you have been involved in over the past years. For each initiative, successful or not, record what went right, what went wrong, and what your role was. Think specifically how you contributed to the level of success achieved.

- Is there anything you could have done better or differently?

- Did you take the opportunity to volunteer for additional responsibilities?

- Did you provide full support to the team?

- Did you deliver your highest quality work?

- Did you have the necessary skills to carry out the work?

- What was your attitude and how did you show up during the project?

- Were you fully committed to its success?

- How did you present yourself?

Use your vantage of better clarity from the self-awareness and social awareness exercise to extract relevant information from this work history. Take the time and make the effort to use your own work history like a post-implementation project assessment. A look-back exercise, especially with the added benefit of 20/20 hindsight, will uncover hidden gems in your history. Being clear here, not all the gems you uncover will be positive. Knowing what did not work and determining what was lacking affords priceless insights and are gems in their own right.

The third list to make may be painful, but it may excavate the most precious of gems. For this list, note times when you proactively sought a leadership role or offered to make a significant contribution, but did not receive the blessings from those in power. This list is not to air old grievances. It is to determine, again from the vantage of your new and improved self-awareness and social awareness perspective, why you were overlooked.

Capture in your notebook why you think you would have been a good choice and why you think your underappreciated idea deserved more consideration. Note why you think you were not perceived as a good choice. What attributes did the chosen person or idea exhibit that you or your idea might have lacked? As much as possible, monitor the assumptions you are making based on emotions and try to stay as objective as possible.

Even after an objective review, you may uncover causes that were and are outside your control. Please know that in the S.H.I.F.T. framework, it is necessary to focus on areas you can influence. Be reassured that you will expand your sphere of influence as you follow the steps laid out in the book.

The hidden gems search in these self-assessments requires great honesty with yourself. As you ponder these experiences now, what do you see that you could have done differently that could have changed the outcome? It might not be "one thing" that would have changed the course. The goal of this excavation is to continue addressing your weaknesses and polishing your strengths.

Some organizations use a performance improvement plan to document steps an employee needs to take to show progress. The document will clearly illustrate what the employee needs to start doing, stop doing, and continue doing to show performance gains in a set time period. The **start, stop, and continue plan** is what you will have at the end of the exercises in this section. This is the personal audit step to ensure you are ready to address any weak links, shore up your strengths, and adopt new practices to increase your probability for success. This step alone has the potential to accelerate your goal accomplishment timeframe.

If immediate tangible benefits often serve as motivators to sustain an improvement journey for you, the rest of the chapter has the potential to give you that by narrowing and sharpening your focus. Most of the other steps in this book need a longer-term commitment. Take the time to stop, reflect, and focus on each prompt. Document your answers in your notebook. These are prompts to narrow and sharpen your focus.

- What specific feedback have you received on prior performances that has stayed with you? Note both the praise and the areas flagged for improvement.

- Do your coworkers come to you for assistance? Is it often related to one area?

- Are you periodically thanked and appreciated by your boss or your peers? Is it often related to a single trait or skill?

- Have you heard an observation about yourself from coworkers more than once? Did they say you were funny, great to collaborate with, or generous with your time? Maybe they casually remarked that you were always late or that you never responded to messages in a timely manner.

- Do your coworkers listen to your ideas when you share them? If not, why not?

- Do you make friends easily at work?

- Did you get overlooked for a promotion more than once? Did you share your concern? What was the response?

- Are you finding it hard to break through into a leadership role? Do you have ideas on what needs to happen?

- What habits are you proud of? Where do you stumble when it comes to consistency?

- What does success look like to you? Why?

- Do you try to stay abreast of activities outside your department? Do you keep up with your industry? Do you review your company's earnings report at least at a cursory level? If your response was a "no" on all three, you may want to fix that if career advancement is what you are pursuing.

To enhance the exercise of excavation you just wrapped up, consider the hidden gem examples from my own professional growth trek and that of my clients and mentees. Perhaps the gems revealed here will expand your view and fill gaps in your own recounting of prior experiences. Consider these, but let your own work history serve as a reference and stay in the foreground as you read ahead. Here are five examples of finding one issue to focus on and then finding tools and resources to overcome it.

Example 1: This is from a coaching client who was struggling to convince his manager that he was worthy of a promotion. His boss cleverly avoided the topic every time it was raised. During our work-history gem exploration sessions, it became obvious my client lacked consistency in couple of areas. We narrowed in on a lack of both timely communication and proactiveness in daily operations. He was good sometimes, but dropped the ball on several occasions. Recognizing this, my client knew what he needed to do: focus on dependable communication and demonstrate consistent proactive habits in daily operations. His new focus on these issues made a huge difference in the perception of others. Good practices applied occasionally rarely yield desired results. Consistency is the name of the game. There are many books on creating good habits. My favorite one is *Atomic Habits* by James Clear.

Example 2: Here's an example from my own hidden gem excavation exercise. Early in my corporate years, I was often asked to repeat what I just said in a conversation. I knew I had an unfamiliar accent, which might be described as a hybrid Indian, British, and American accent. It wasn't my pace of communication. I had slowed down my rate of speech to be respectful to my colleagues. Those requests to repeat myself made me feel less competent and left me frustrated. To address this weakness, I found a speech/voice coach. That was an invaluable investment. I discovered the issue was not the accent but the emphasis on the wrong stress syllable. I practiced what I learned from my speech coach and stayed intentional during conversations. I have not heard a request to repeat myself in years.

Example 3: One of my mentees had received poor feedback on his verbal communication skills. His communication lacked clarity and focus. He was told that he took too long to get to the point. Often when people can't comprehend your message, it's an indication of muddled thinking or an inability to stay with a single thread or train of thought. Most of us at some point in our careers have been confronted with this issue. After I suggested that he read quality authors, listen to professional podcasts, and adopt a regular writing practice to express his thoughts on paper, his ability to stay on point tangibly improved in a very short period. His focus on this one issue yielded a fast turnaround success story.

Example 4: A coaching client was frustrated about her inability to break into a leadership role. She was convinced that she had the necessary skills, but promotions were not coming her way. We worked to develop her leadership presence, and I gently nudged her to seek out a mentor from the senior leadership ranks at work. She was amazed by the company-specific insights she received from her mentor. Her grasp of the influence and authority structures in her company was greatly enhanced by this productive partnership. She now believes that she can navigate her career advancement strategy effectively. What you may not know is that most leaders in your company would be thrilled to mentor you. All you need to do is ask respectfully.

Example 5: This last example is also a personal one. During my corporate career days, people often left a conversation with me with a remark like "I was feeling down when I called you for advice, and I feel so much better now." Initially, I just smiled and was happy that I could brighten someone's day. Much later during a phase of deep reflection, I realized I had an innate talent for coaching, and motivating. When I was ready to make a career switch, I leveraged this hidden gem in my history to make a meaningful and appropriate career shift. So, here is an important question for you to consider. Are you paying attention to comments about you offered in an off-the-cuff way?

Using these five examples as a reference, study the notes you captured in the earlier exercise. Treasure the gems you uncovered that show where you need work. Now you can take action to turn them either neutral or even into a strength. Embrace the success-oriented gems you uncovered and work toward deploying them more often. Take a few minutes and start writing down the next steps to shore up your key positives and address the impactful negatives. Addressing them may include books, courses, workshops, coaching sessions, and more. Write down the areas you would like to address and how you plan to address them. When you are assessing your experiences, think about these three topics:

- **Courage** — Have you considered what your lack of courage is costing you? I used to ask this question of myself every time I had an aching sense that I must do something, anything, to propel me out of an untenable or unproductive situation. Have you considered the cost of being stuck or frozen? Sometimes it is a single act of courage that helps you get unstuck, but more often it is an incremental approach to consistently practice courage where we take small steps outside our comfort zone. We all know that our comfort zone is the greatest threat to us living our potential. How you challenge yourself every day to push through your discomfort is essential to developing your courage muscle. *Our brains are wired to discount the cost of inaction and to overestimate the probability of failure.* Daniel Kahneman described Loss Aversion in detail in his book *Thinking, Fast and Slow*. Fight the impulse to always play it safe in a work meeting or in a conversation with the boss. If you don't venture, you will not gain. In other words, no risk, no glory. How do you push past your comfort zone?

- **Vibes** — What is your vibe at work? Do you signal you are rushed, frustrated, uninterested? Do the signals you send attract or repel your coworkers when it comes to engaging with you? What might you need to adjust in the signals you are sending based on how people are responding to you? This is called out in the social awareness segment of the prior chapter. A client was raised in a culture where open and direct talk was the norm. That resulted in a straight-shooting no-nonsense style of communication at work. That style of communication was unfortunately sending out unintended vibes. Sometimes, the directness was perceived as rude. We worked to help her soften her style to an indirect approach that gave her team members some space to arrive at the desired conclusion instead of her always serving it up directly. You might not have been aware of the signals you were sending, but now with your attention on self-awareness and social awareness, you are alert and present in everyday conversations. Adopt a generous spirit, show kindness, and always connect with the right intention when you walk into an uncomfortable situation. You can flip the script with good intentions and a generous spirit. All is not lost.

- **Success** — Your definition of success in the past may not have been entirely your own. You may have borrowed it from others and sadly that took you on the wrong path. For example, a friend of mine always thought an international traveling job would be amazing because she watched others go to exciting or exotic destinations. All she could imagine was experiencing lovely destinations and rich cultures for herself. When she finally got that coveted job, it was nothing like she imagined. The hours spent in airports were bad enough, but working through jetlag was sheer misery. What she imagined her dream job to be was a job that left her listless. With what you have uncovered in your work so far, examine your definition of success. Think about what satisfies you, what makes you feel most proud, what work carries the most significance to you, what makes you happy. This can help you get to your definition of success for your future self.

Spend some time reading and organizing your notes on hidden gems. Highlight all the areas that need additional examination. Identify areas that need input from other sources. Did you discover that it would be helpful to take a course to overcome a skill gap or to achieve mastery in an area that is one of your strengths? Did you determine that working with a coach could benefit you? This may be a lot to process. Sit with this for a while and think about it. What action(s) are you willing to take?

As you get nearer to execution steps in your transformation plan, there is one common gem to consider that affects a large population of the workforce: poor time management.

Know Your Time

Time is the scarcest of all resources. Handle it with care. You are dealing with an extraordinary number of demands placed on you. You are juggling high-priority tasks, responding to crisis emails, keeping your boss updated, putting out fires at work, and, above all, ensuring you are on top of all your responsibilities at home. Did I get that right?

I can clearly recall falling onto my couch at eight thirty in the evening to watch a few sitcoms to unwind and within ten minutes, I would have fallen asleep. Often on a Friday afternoon, I would look back after wrapping up a crazy busy week with no lunch breaks and be shocked at how I managed to skip my own high priority items. I let other people's agendas drive my own. While we have to work as a team, we also need to keep an eye on our priorities, the areas that need our focus and attention. Is it any wonder that burnout is now a part of our everyday vocabulary?

When you were in school, your days were scheduled for you. You were given defined blocks of time to devote to one subject at a time. The need to constantly have your brain shift gears was not necessary. As an adult, you set your own schedule but often abandon it to accommodate new requests for your time. Switching gears constantly hurts your performance and productivity.

Often, we hear the excuse of a lack of time to get important things done. Could it be a lack of prioritization that is the culprit? As Zig Ziglar noted, "Lack of direction, not lack of time, is the problem. We all have twenty-four-hour days."

Have you ever wondered how some of your peers get a lot more done with the same number of hours? Somehow, they never ask for an extension of a deadline or look harried and stressed. Could it be that they are clear on their priorities and their most important goals?

The first time I heard about a time management method was during a class offered by my employer in the mid-90s. It was the most impactful one of that year. The method was Franklin Covey's Time Management matrix with its four quadrants. It's sometimes referred to as The Eisenhower Matrix. Look it up on the web if you are curious to learn more. It's a time and priority management method I use every week on Sunday afternoon to organize my week for maximum productivity by urgency and importance. To use the tool, you'll place your weekly/monthly tasks and activities in one of the four quadrants.

- Quadrant 1 is for **urgent and important** tasks. These are significant obligations or activities that are important in nature and demand immediate attention.

- Quadrant 2 is for **important but not urgent** tasks. These activities are essential to your personal growth. These are often related to goals you set for yourself. When you fail to follow through on your personal goals, it's often this quadrant that is sidelined. **Your future self needs your attention to stay on this quadrant.**

- Quadrant 3 is for **urgent but not important tasks**. Items that fall here are generally significant only for a short period of time. The importance of these tasks is frequently determined by the priorities of others. You may be swayed to move a task that belongs here in Quadrant 3 into your Quadrant 1. That is when your productivity suffers. Brenden Burchard, a top-rated high-performance coach, says that emails are a task list of other people's priorities. If you tackle emails first thing in the morning, you will move into this quadrant without planning for items that are important to you in your first and second quadrant. One way to manage these urgent but not important tasks is to deal with them in a defined block of time outside of your peak activity period.

- Quadrant 4 is **not important and not urgent**. These tasks are more likely here to serve a purpose, and this may be the right time for you to question that purpose. These may be activities that you enjoy but are not aligned with your career goals. These tasks could be basic downtime activities after a busy day. It is essential to unwind at the end of the day for your overall well-being. Having fun every day is also recommended, but it doesn't have to be at the expense of you living your potential. Tasks in this quadrant often may be aligned to wasteful and non-productive habits like doom scrolling on social media. There was a period in my life when I would just turn on the TV as a practice in the morning. The day I decided "no TV until six p.m.," my creative projects blossomed. I dedicated my morning hours to personal growth and hobbies. Everyone needs time to unwind and de-stress. Quadrant 4 activities, not urgent and not important, should serve a specific purpose and not occupy the productive hours of your day. Manage them effectively.

To help you reduce stress and manage your time more constructively, identify tasks, actions, or activities that are helpful to your growth and career advancement (Quadrant 2). Career advancement tasks could be work projects where your output has a positive impact on the organization and increases your perceived value. Pick a color to highlight them when you add them to your calendar. Next, identify categories that are unhelpful to your growth and career advancement. These could be meetings you attend that serve no purpose for example. If you think it makes you more visible in the organization, it rarely does. The impact you make when you deliver important work to the right audience is what raises your visibility. Pick a color to highlight low value-add activities. This lets you see at a glance when your focus waivers.

If you don't document every activity on your calendar, start doing that now for four weeks or go back and fill in the gaps in your calendar. Checking your old emails will help with some of the gaps. Evaluate your calendar with the time matrix in the foreground. Look for blocks that left you with a sense of accomplishment and those that left you depleted.

With the above activity complete, here are a few questions for you to ponder. Write the responses in your notebook.

- Do you attend meetings where you have nothing to contribute? Will you gain something in the meeting that you cannot glean from meeting notes?

- Do you constantly rearrange and prioritize tasks throughout the day? If yes, why?

- Do you constantly shift gears from one task to another because of a new request? If yes, why?

- Are you inventing things to do to avoid the difficult but important things? This one happens all too often. Be watchful!

- If you are a manager or team lead, do you delegate? If not, why not.

- If you are a manager or team lead, do you evaluate the purpose and objectives of your meetings and those of your team members? Most employees in recent polls have attributed the feeling of overwhelm to hours spent in non-productive meetings.

At least three times a day stop and ask yourself, am I being productive or just busy? No matter where you are in your time management journey, know that there are methods, resources, and tools to help you get better with allocating your time. Choose one that aligns with your work to help with prioritization, organization, deadlines, and recording and analyzing your time. You may be like me and choose to keep it simple and just use your current calendar app and maximize its utility. Better time management leads to greater career success and quality downtime every day. You even get breaks in your day to refresh and recharge. Get comfortable saying no to unimportant things.

Here's one last **productivity tip**. There are certain kinds of tasks that are often procrastinated and somehow they manage to hang over your head every day. You think about them in the morning, you think about them during the day, and they are the last thing you think about before you go to bed. They often fall into quick tasks like sending a one-off difficult email or calling someone. The trick is to address this kind of task first thing in the morning. Get it done, and it loses its hold on you and your creativity. Sometimes the procrastinated task is a sizable project that you know you need to tackle, but the very size of it overwhelms you. Take some time to divide the task into chunks and tackle one chunk at a time. Even getting a small part done feels liberating and frees you to focus on other important tasks stress-free.

Is there anything you can rearrange in your calendar for the next week by practicing these skills? Maybe you can add a few reminders to help you stay on track. This is one of the immediate tangible benefits I promised earlier in this chapter.

Just as poor time management stalls your progress, so does poor fear management. That is where you will work next.

Manage Your Fears

Think back on your history again and this time identify fears that have held you back. Was it the fear of failure, fear of rejection, fear of uncertainty, or possibly the fear of success?

Your important goals can scare you. They can require you to call on your courage and your wisdom to overcome your fears. There is no room for letting fear win in your success journey. It is incumbent upon you to leave the safety of the familiar if you want to create opportunities that will help you live your potential. Of course, you should always consider risks in your evaluation and assessment prior to taking the leap, but you should equally consider the **cost of inaction.** Just take a moment to consider all your lost opportunities because you surrendered to your fears and refused to leave the safety of the familiar. Most of us are very good at considering what might go wrong, but rarely do we consider the cost of settling for the status quo. Don't let yourself fall into that trap.

Don't assume failure before you even start. Don't decide you have no shot at a promotion, so you never ask or apply for a job. Don't play it safe. Don't stay silent when you have input to contribute on the off chance that others might not agree or that you might look foolish. Don't let fear overpower you. That's when another coworker sweeps in and steals your thunder.

> *Everything you want is on the other side of fear.* — **Jack Canfield**

Much of our suffering comes from unfounded fears. Early in my career, I tended to choose the safe options, which prevented me from doing things essential for my growth. My husband gave me a wise question to ask when I was in the grip of anxiety: what is the worst that can happen?

I took that one step further and created a pros and cons list before stepping outside my comfort zone. As I built that list, I'd walk through scenarios and evaluate the probability of each occurring and its impact if it did. Watching this play out on paper definitely helped quell many of my unfounded worries.

Consider watching Tim Ferriss's TedTalk[1] on "fear setting." It is a well-organized exercise you may want to try when you are stalling on an important action. Essentially the purpose of fear setting is to systematically analyze a situation that you fear.

---
1 Tim Ferriss. Why you should define your fears instead of your goals. TEDTalk July 14, 2017. https://www.youtube.com/watch?v=5J6jAC6XxAI.

To summarize and slightly modify Tim Ferriss's approach, make a list of worst things that could happen if you took a certain action or made a certain decision. This could be something big like asking for a promotion or making a formal complaint or something smaller like speaking up in a meeting. In a second column, list what you could do to prevent that feared outcome from happening. In a third column capture the actions you can take preemptively to decrease the likelihood of the scenario happening. The fourth and last column is to capture the actions needed if the worst did happen.

At this point, you can see ways to recognize your fears, assess their impact if they did happen to occur, and have a plan to mitigate them. There's one more step. Now consider and list what the upside might be if you did take that risk, overcame the fear, and took action. The benefits uncovered in this last step and their associated value are what the *cost of inaction* represents for you.

On some occasions, you may conclude that your fear is well-founded and go no further, but more often it is likely that the upside might pull you more strongly, and you decide the fears are just an unnecessary roadblock you created. Using a systematic approach like this will make hard choices easier. Use an approach like this anytime you are struggling with an apparent risky decision.

The reason I called out fear in the S.H.I.F.T. framework is because it has the greatest potential to derail your best plans. You need moments of reflection to consider pros and cons, and you need an approach to visualize and assess a situation objectively. If not, your fears may continue to have a hold on you. Don't allow any spiraling thoughts of poor outcomes to immobilize you. If the vision of your future self is strong, then do this analytical work so you can move forward.

If you feel you have captured some observations from your prior challenging experiences in your notebook, you are ready to move to the next consideration. The last hidden gem, unlike poor time management and poor fear management, can be hard to discover on your own.

Morning routine

Just imagine that you are asked to organize an event or lead a project. Would you start executing it without knowing the objective of the event or project? No, I don't think so. The objective, the desired outcome, is a primary consideration when drawing up a plan to execute. But so often we go through our daily activities without a clear objective or intention or plan. When we start our day without an objective and intention, we start operating on autopilot as the day progresses. We let others own our agenda, time, and productivity.

A simple morning routine to set your intention for the day can change all of that overnight. You take back control by centering yourself, focusing on your goals, and setting the intention for the day. Titans of industry and thought leaders attribute their success to their morning routine. They meditate, they journal, they get clear on their intentions for the day, and they exercise. If it takes waking up before sunrise, they do it, because they know the value of this daily practice. Reading about their journeys is what inspired me to adopt a morning routine of my own.

For me, the most beneficial part of my morning routine is journaling. I tried freehand journaling for a while, but soon noticed that I wasn't consistent. On some days it felt hard to write down my thoughts. Without consistency, the effectiveness of my action would be limited. Then I discovered a YouTube-recommended video that talked up the value of *The Five Minute Journal*. It turned out to be a gift from the universe, a real game-changer. It's a journal for those who do not like journaling. If you don't have time to journal or feel like you can't maintain a freehand journaling habit, I encourage you to get this journal from *Intelligentchange.com* now. For the last five years or so, I have been gifting this amazing life-changing journal to close friends and family. If I were Oprah Winfrey, this journal would be on my Favorite Things list year after year.

The journal helps you center yourself, especially if your mind starts churning stories early in the morning. With its short, crisp prompts, this journal is based on proven positive psychology research. In just five minutes a day, it trains your mind to focus on the good in your life. There are prompts for the start of your new day. And there are prompts for the evening before you retire for the night. Responding to the prompts conditions your brain to focus on the positive. You reflect on the good things that happened throughout your day and think how you can improve tomorrow. Prompts ask you to name things you are grateful for or things you could do to make the day great. There are affirmation statements too. The evening prompts have you reflect on what was great in the day or what you could have done better. The creators of this journal claim that it is the simplest, most effective thing you can do every day to be happier. I agree simply because there is no denying the results it has brought me.

Before I adopted a morning routine, I allowed limiting beliefs and unhappy narratives to take over my mind. Those stories left me feeling tense and more reactive to everyday interactions. My relationships at work did not feel satisfying or productive. I felt stressed, anxious, and on edge. I often felt I was surrounded by takers and not givers. I would catastrophize and see the glass as half empty. I was probably labeled a pessimist or a Negative Nelly by those who knew me well.

But here is the remarkable news. When you train your mind to see the positive and appreciate the small wonders, your behavior and attitude change. After my morning routine was established, my perspective and attitude transformed. I was present in conversations and laughed a lot more at work. My negative "woe is me" stories were miraculously gone. I stopped giving them oxygen by setting my positive intention for the day.

I threw myself into service and started thinking creatively about my life and purpose. When I focused on the positive, my happiness level improved, and my demeanor at work was steady, in control, and calm. Nearly all work relationships were productive and enjoyable. Sadly, you will always come up against a few self-serving individuals at work. Know that the power plays will continue, but your morning routine will protect you and leave you unscathed.

In my opinion, a morning routine is the one practice that lets you take back control of your mission. It reminds you of your goals and centers you with positive thoughts. No matter the distraction, a sound morning routine will keep you on track. Here's a great quote from the book *The Art of Possibility*:

> *Thank you for reminding me what I am here for. I will have to remember "I am here today to cross the swamp, not to fight all the alligators."* — **Rosamund Stone Zander and Benjamin Zander**

How often do you get caught up in fighting alligators—distractions like unnecessary meetings, surprise work items, breaking news stories, social media, conflicts, office politics—when you are trying to get to the other side of the swamp? Let your time allocation quadrants, your fear management techniques, and your morning routine help you set your priorities, give you courage, and build a positive mindset.

Congratulations! You have taken another major leap forward. Harnessing the hidden gems from your history has brought your next steps into sharper focus and has given you greater clarity, confidence, and courage to execute them. Take a moment to savor the work you have done and the new understanding you have gained. Your next step in S.H.I.F.T. is to Ignite Your Power!

CHAPTER SUMMARY _____

- With the benefit of 20/20 hindsight, focus on the lessons that come from your work history.

- Living your potential can become a reality when you take ownership and manage your time and your fears well.

- The most effective way to create satisfying and fulfilling days is establishing a morning routine.

CHAPTER 5

IGNITE YOUR POWER

This is the step you likely have been waiting for because it shifts the focus from preparation to action. In this chapter you will identify the goals with the greatest potential for impact, call them out in a plan, and start task execution.

First, a word about the power within you. We all have some level of personal power. We use our power in our unique ways to influence people and events. This power comes from our foundational core, which includes our values, our confidence, our courage, our curiosity, and other individual characteristics rather than any formal authority bestowed on us. Someone with a strong sense of power has a heightened capacity to regulate themselves and relate to others. You focused on those themes of self-efficacy and connection in the earlier chapters. In this chapter, you will ignite your personal power and elevate the work you are doing. Your sense of self, your self-worth, your people skills, and your achievements will undergo a renovation, still uniquely you, but better. This is the fuel you need to power through what comes next. I know you can't wait to get started on your goals!

By this point in your journey, you have completed the exercises related to self-awareness and social awareness. You have uncovered hidden gems from your history, including the essentials of time management, fear management, and adopting a transformational morning routine practice. You have made such progress!

Review your notes along this journey, revisit your vision for your future self, and **write a short summary** of what you would like to focus on based on the gems you have uncovered and the work you have already completed. Following that review and the summary exercise, **create a list** of specific areas that would make a significant impact on your career trajectory and simultaneously fulfill you. Number the list with one being your highest priority area. Your work now will focus on setting goals to get you to that destination or to accomplish that desired objective.

Goal Setting

There are different approaches to setting goals. The approach you choose will depend some on personal preference but more on the nature of your goal and what it will take to achieve it. Three goal-setting methods are presented here: SMART goals, future identity goals, and a hybrid of the two.

- You likely have heard of **SMART** goals. This approach to goal creation emphasizes the importance of goals being specific, measurable, achievable, relevant, and time-bound. Without measurement, it is hard to gauge progress toward a goal. Metrics and milestones promote progress and, more importantly, they help sustain your motivation levels.

- **FUTURE IDENTITY** goals are based on how your future self will show up at work every day. This can include the skills your future self will have and the values your future self will exhibit. Your work is to strive to attain those traits and (or) become aligned with your future values. This approach works very well when you are trying to master soft skills. For example, if your future identity has a calmer and less intense personality, you need to start practicing those attributes and traits every day with intentionality, starting now.

- For some, a **HYBRID** approach may be most effective. You may have two goals to accomplish, a soft skill and a hard skill. You may use the Future Identity model for the soft skill and for a technical hard skill you choose the boundaries and clarity afforded by **SMART** goals. What you are striving for is a desired destination and a plan on how to get there.

Put reasonable parameters around your initial goals to increase your odds of getting to your target, and then you can iteratively build on that success with confidence.

- Set this round of goals to no more than a year out from a timeline perspective. A possible exception to this set time is something like earning a degree or a special certification. Know that you will build on your initial success and execute on your big, hairy, audacious goals, otherwise known as BHAG goals in the last step of Thrive and Flourish in the S.H.I.F.T. framework. Desmond Tutu once noted that the only way to eat an elephant is one bite at a time. Everything in life that seems daunting, overwhelming, and even impossible can be accomplished gradually by taking on a little at a time. Work on first things first, then move on.

- Ideally, do not attempt more than two or three goals at this point in your growth journey. A good mix would be two professional goals and one personal goal. The objective of this limit on the number of goals is to increase your odds of success. Succeeding will help you experience the high of accomplishing your set targets and make you come alive. With that comes a happier you showing up at work. That is an extremely important outcome, because your positivity and pleasant disposition will make you a people magnet. With that comes opportunities for better connections at work. You can now see how elements of this larger framework are connected. You do not want to take on too much at one time and burn out or stress out. It is easy to underestimate how much time—and effort— is needed to get something accomplished. You also have your current work, home responsibilities, and your social network to take care of.

Here is an example of three goals:

1. **Professional – SOFT SKILL:** Have better conversations at work
   a. **Action:** Practice communicating in a gentle yet persuasive way
   b. **Action:** Be aware of body language and voice tone
   c. **Action:** Practice active listening

2. **Professional – SOFT SKILL:** Become a more effective delegator
   a. **Action:** Dedicate time every day to managing priorities
   b. **Action:** Break down tasks into actionable pieces for better delegation
   c. **Action:** Look for opportunities to delegate every day

3. **Personal:** Better health
   a. **Action:** Commit to a one-hour walk six days a week
   b. **Action:** Develop better sleep hygiene to improve quality of sleep

By keeping it simple and limited to three goals, setting your intentionality for the day also becomes easier and so does the consistent application of skills and traits that support your goal. During your morning routine, write down your intentions in your *Five Minute Journal* or notebook and enter reminders on your calendar. It should take no more than 10 minutes every day.

The following are more examples and generalizations to help you consider possible scenarios for your goal setting exercise. Your goals may be similar or be entirely different.

A. If you are focused on career advancement in your current company, your goals may read something like this:

1. **Professional – SOFT SKILL:** Work toward a promotion next year
   a. **Action:** Obtain guidance from a mentor
   b. **Action:** Be intentional and showcase leadership skills at work
   c. **Action:** Socialize my leadership skills and my results via tactful emails and conversations

2. **Professional and Personal – SOFT SKILL:** Become more productive
   a. **Action:** Schedule time on my calendar for a weekly task prioritization activity (use the Covey Matrix for guidance if needed)
   b. **Action:** Review priorities and actions daily to ensure adherence to plan

3. **Personal:** Schedule quality "Me Time"
   a. **Action:** Say no to invitations and distractions that take me away from my objective
   b. **Action:** Set aside an hour every evening for reading and reflecting

B. If you had chosen an accounting, HR, or project management certification for career advancement, your goals may read something like this:

   1. **Professional – HARD SKILL:** Earn a professional certification
      a. **Action:** Set time on my calendar to work on course material and take practice tests
      b. **Action:** Address the individual certification requirements
      c. **Action:** While I am learning, apply new knowledge/skills to my work

   2. **Professional and Personal – SOFT SKILL:** Practice better time management
      a. **Action:** Be clear on my priorities for the day
      b. **Action:** Handle my routine email in a block of time twice a day

   3. **Personal:** Plan a vacation for the family
      a. **Action:** Decide on vacation destination
      b. **Action:** Make reservations
      c. **Action:** Plan a few activities but leave plenty of time for relaxation

C. A hidden gem you may have identified during your exploration in the previous chapter could be your work with Excel. That expertise is regularly recognized by your peers and manager. Could you take it to mastery level for a larger impact? That could become your core differentiator and your unique selling proposition. It would expand your sphere of influence. You would no longer just be helping your team; your assistance would be sought by other functional areas in your organization.

1. **Professional – HARD SKILL:** Master Advanced Excel
   a. **Action:** Schedule time on my calendar for Excel mastery
   b. **Action:** Learn course material and take practice tests
   c. **Action:** Apply new skills on the job

2. **Personal:** Daily practice of my passion—singing
   a. **Action:** Spend one hour every morning on my vocal exercises

D. You enjoy your job and believe your leadership team is impressed with your work. You have delivered significant results, and you have enhanced your leadership skills. You are convinced that your salary does not match the value you offer. You are confident that this is the right time to negotiate a salary increase with your manager. Your goals may read like this:

1. **Professional – SOFT SKILL:** Prepare for a salary negotiation in the next four months
   a. **Action:** Collect performance evidence like project metrics and emails expressing gratitude and praise for my work
   b. **Action:** Get advice on negotiation best practices from a negotiator in my professional network or

YouTube negotiation professionals recognized as experts in their field
   c. **Action:** Interview for a new job to present job/salary offer as evidence of my fair market rate

2. **Professional – SOFT SKILL:** Networking and relationship building
   a. **Action:** Schedule one hour a week to network with peers in the industry
   b. **Action:** Get curious and apply social awareness insights to build better relationships

These examples should have given you ideas and inspiration to get started on defining your goals and setting action items. Take the time now to set your own two to three goals and identify the actions you will take to work toward them. The examples given were necessarily generic to give you a general idea of their use, but know that the more focused and specific you are in setting your goals and specifying your actions, the better your results will be. Once you have your goals set (and remember, they can be adjusted as needed later), then review the following prelaunch checklist to make sure you are ready to go!

Prelaunch Checklist

Plan to dedicate at least an hour to your key priorities every day.

1. Have you set a time of the day to dedicate to furthering your goals? *Note: Remember you can practice your*

skills throughout the day. *This one hour is dedicated to learning.*

2. Do you have a plan to manage your priorities and your time? It could be using your current calendar, an Excel spreadsheet, or another time management option. When will you schedule time for weekly prioritization? Sunday afternoon is when I prioritize because it is the calmest and quietest part of my week. Schedule a 30-minute slot in your calendar for weekly prioritizations now.

3. Have you purchased or borrowed books that can help you with your specific goals?

4. Have you signed up for courses or coaching you need for your specific goals?

5. Have you notified your accountability partner that you are kicking off your execution step?

6. Do you have a tool to track your progress? *Note: My work calendar also served as my tracker. You can track in a notebook, Excel, or any other tool of your choice.*

7. Do you have a risk mitigation plan to overcome doubts and fears that bubble up in your journey? *Note: It could be creating a pros and cons list of "what if" scenarios by asking "what is the worst that can happen" or an evaluation of the cost of inaction. Circle back to the section on managing your fears if you are unsure.*

8. Have you thought about an approach to come back to your goals after an unforeseen delay or setback? If not, write that down. *Note: Always be kind to yourself and know that life happens and setbacks are mostly temporary intrusions.*

9. Do you have a plan to celebrate weekly wins?
    a. **IMPORTANT:** The early weeks of any focused effort toward a goal are very lonely. You don't necessarily appreciate the change your effort is bringing about until someone else notices. That recognition is the fuel for your onward journey. When you are chasing a growth objective, it can take a while before results are noticed by others. It may cause you to want to give up, but don't. This is the perfect time to bring up the bamboo tree.

    The seed of a bamboo tree is extremely hard when planted. The seed will do nothing for almost five years. All you will see is the dirt covering it. Nothing happens in the first year or the second, not the third or the fourth. You have to faithfully water that spot of dirt for years. That is, until the fifth year. In the fifth year, the seed sprouts, breaks through the soil, and begins to grow into a tree. It grows 3 feet a day, almost 90 feet in about a month. Now, just imagine if the caretaker had abandoned that seed in the dirt.

    That is why it is extremely important that you track consistency and not outcomes when you are playing the long game. Celebrating wins in the consistency arena will let you know that you are making progress like that caretaker of the bamboo seed. Make it a practice to review your weekly calendar or tracker late on a Friday afternoon and celebrate your consistent and dedicated effort that week.

When I am on a mission, I have a Friday four p.m. reminder on my calendar to check in and evaluate. A weekly win is entered in my notebook. A colleague of mine chose to commemorate her wins with certificates of accomplishment. Four straight weeks of wins earned her a certificate. She created it using a Word certificate template and saved it in her growth folder. When her enthusiasm and commitment levels dropped, she would review her accumulated certificates to appreciate how far she had come. You could try this approach or an approach that is better suited for you. How you celebrate is entirely up to you. For example, it could be a fancy dinner with your spouse, a new box of your favorite golf balls, a mani-pedi appointment, or a fancy coffee. Obviously, the week where you feel you missed the mark, do not reward yourself. If punitive measures work with your psychology, go a step further and set up a penalty that is really annoying to you.

If you answered yes to all nine questions in the prelaunch checklist above, congratulations! You are ready to hit the accelerator. Let's go. Your future is calling. I hope you are as moved and inspired by this quote as I am:

You were born with wings.
You were not meant for crawling, so don't.
You have wings. Learn to use them and fly.
—**Rumi**

Execution Approach

The execution approach I am sharing here is the approach my clients, mentees, and I adopted. You can tweak it to suit your lifestyle and specific goals. Reminder: Course correction is recommended when facts on the ground change.

Once-a-week tasks

- Weekly prioritization

    o Identify your top three activities to work on this week. At least two of the three activities should be related to the goals you set earlier in this chapter. A work priority is often on this weekly prioritization list.

    o Enter reminders in your calendar for every day of the week.

- Celebrate your weekly wins

    o Set aside time to review your progress in terms of consistency. Friday afternoons are fantastic for that review. Log your wins and celebrate.

Daily Commitment and Execution

Adopting accelerators for growth as a daily practice will get you to live your true potential a lot sooner than if they are treated as nice-to-do occasional actions. There are **five recommended accelerators** listed here. This may feel overwhelming at first. They are ordered in a way to enhance your journey and results. Accelerator 1 is building the habit of consistency as you execute steps needed for your specific goals. Accelerators 2 through 5 will need no additional scheduled time on your calendar. Isn't knowing that a relief? Believe me, I know your calendar cannot hold any more tasks. The only requirement is understanding the utility of accelerators 2 through 5. When practiced regularly and consistently, these accelerators will become natural for you. Their purpose is to enrich your daily experiences at work, bring you joy, and lower risk on the path to the implementation of PROJECT YOU!

To begin with, adopt ONLY the first three accelerators as a practice for **four weeks** and watch your energy and vitality shift. The daily execution will be simple if you commit to staying present, mindful, and intentional. Consistent application of these practices for four weeks will increase the probability of sustaining these best practices for life as they do become a natural part of your personality.

After four weeks, you can then move on to adopting practices for accelerators 4 and 5 into your daily routine.

The reward you will receive for the proper application of these accelerators is priceless. The confidence you exhibit at work will be palpable and experienced by everyone around you.

Weeks one through four

Accelerator 1: Consistency – This is about ensuring your focus and attention are on your top goals and that you are executing the needed steps every day. The **goals** you defined earlier fall within this accelerator. The accelerators that follow are designed to ensure you are elevating your personal power.

> *We are what we repeatedly do. Excellence, then, is not an act, but a habit.* — **Will Durant**

For example, as illustrated in the example earlier in the chapter, if these three were your goals, you will get started on these three as a part of the adoption of accelerator 1.

1. **Professional – HARD SKILL:** Earn a professional certification
   a. **Action:** Set time on my calendar to work on course material and take practice tests
   b. **Action:** Address the individual certification requirements
   c. **Action:** While I am learning, apply new knowledge/skills to my work

2. **Professional and Personal – SOFT SKILL:** Practice better time management
   a. **Action:** Be clear on my priorities for the day

  b. **Action:** Handle my routine email in a block of time twice a day

3. **Personal:** Plan a vacation for the family
  a. **Action:** Decide on vacation destination
  b. **Action:** Make reservations
  c. **Action:** Plan a few activities but leave plenty of time for relaxation

For goal 1, you will schedule time on your calendar to review requirements and course material, study and practice taking tests, and apply new skills learned in your daily work activities. You will do something every day to move you forward on this goal.

For goal 2, you will follow through on prioritization and block time for specific tasks to increase productivity. You will do something every day to move forward on this goal.

For goal 3, you will dedicate time on your calendar for family conversations to decide on a vacation destination and then make necessary reservations. You will take regular action to move yourself forward on this goal.

Accelerator 2: Morning routine – This is about sitting in silence, journaling, setting the intention for the day. A tool like *The Five Minute Journal* will set you up for more productive, joyful, and meaningful days. Setting the intention for the day increases the odds of better choices throughout the day. Better choices increase the possibility of reaching your goal and regular application increases the probability of getting to your goal.

Accelerator 3: Practice round the clock intentionality – In the prior accelerator, you set your intention for the day. Here you take it a step further. Get into the consistent habit of setting intentions before every meeting and every conversation. This is to avoid slipping up and getting into autopilot mode. Think about how you want to show up in meetings at work. Do you want to listen or lead the conversation? Do you want to be perceived as a problem solver or complainer?

Week four and forward

Accelerator 4: Self-Awareness – Look inward every now and then and evaluate your mood, your choices, and your actions. Get curious about yourself. We are all a work-in-progress. It is incumbent on you to learn more about yourself every single day.

Here are a few sample questions to ask yourself:

1. Are you showing up as you intended? If not, why not?

2. Are you choosing comfort over courage? Why? Was it the right choice for this situation?

3. When you feel triggered, why did it happen? What contributed to it? What was the stimulus? Seek the answer. If it was anger, examine the cause. If you were in tears, ask yourself why. If you were irritated, discern why. Being triggered easily makes you reactive. Being reactive causes you to be perceived as weak

and not powerful. This chapter is titled "Ignite Your Power" and being reactive causes the loss of power. Your power lies in how you respond.

Between stimulus and response, there is a space. In that space lies our freedom and our power to choose our response. In our response lies our growth and our happiness. — **Viktor Frankl**

Feel the emotion but do not react. Unproductive emotions at work are an indulgence you should avoid. It's okay to feel the emotions, but practice not being triggered by them.

Your goal is to show emotional control in a workplace if your desire is to rise up the ranks.

4. Are you unknowingly giving out vibes of entitlement? You may rightly believe you are skilled, talented, and resourceful. But with that belief and conviction, an aura of deservedness may take over your demeanor. Nothing annoys your peers and leaders more than a sense of entitlement on full display. Regular practice and commitment to humility will reward you richly.

5. Are distractions derailing your performance? Evaluate and eliminate them.

Accelerator 5: Social Awareness – This accelerator is all about getting curious about others. If you need a quick refresher on social awareness, take a few minutes to read the insights shared in chapter 3. "Works well with others" on an annual report card is something to aspire to.

Here are a few reminders:

1. Look for opportunities to build relationships.

2. Look for opportunities to serve and be helpful.

3. Assume good intentions when you encounter a seemingly uncharitable situation. Know that it is hard to read the intentions of others. This is primarily to keep you centered and to avoid unnecessarily triggering yourself.

4. Read the room. This is important advice I share with my coaching clients. If you are trying to break into the senior ranks of your organization, this reminder is even more critical to you. Before you write an email or share your opinion in a meeting, understand the ambitions and motives of the people in your audience. Don't have blinders on. Don't be oblivious. Don't be paranoid, but do raise your awareness.

   You may share an insight that may make a senior leader uncomfortable because it goes against his desires or her ambition. Your outspokenness, competence, or knowledge might threaten others in the room, so be mindful of unintended consequences. You can still share your opinion and your wisdom, but do it strategically by being fully aware of the influence and authority structures in your organization and in the room. Who has clout and who doesn't? Do not stay invisible and quiet, just be savvy. Spend a little time analyzing the political landscape to execute well enough to give you the outcomes you desire.

Exit Criteria

At the close of the eighth week following the start of your acceleration plan, check your calendar or tracker to answer these questions as honestly as possible.

- Did you consistently work on your key goals in accelerator 1 starting week one?

- Did you consistently work on the objectives of accelerators 2 and 3 starting week one?

- Did you consistently work on the objectives of accelerators 4 and 5 starting week four?

The goal of this section is to build consistent habits and practices. If you answered yes to these questions, know that you are making meaningful and enduring progress. If you have been consistent, you will notice that you have built habits that will sustain well beyond your current journey. You have built the foundation of your successful and fulfilled future self. You can feel your curiosity, courage, confidence, and resolve telling you to march on to bigger and better destinations. I believe that PROJECT YOU is ready to launch. Are you ready to reveal the *new* YOU on Launch Day?

CHAPTER SUMMARY

- Having fewer goals to work with at a time increases focus, does not overwhelm you, and, above all, makes successful outcomes more likely. Success is key to building momentum toward reaching new and more impactful milestones.

- Intentionality and consistency are essential to building good habits, increasing effectiveness, and ensuring the achievement of goals.

- Staying alert and present will keep your self-awareness and social awareness antennae picking up beneficial clues.

CHAPTER 6

FORGE YOUR PATH TO FULFILLMENT

It is Launch Day for PROJECT YOU. You have arrived with the foundational tools and techniques to set you up for success. An improved version of you has been deployed in your workplace.

You must be wondering, how is this day any different? On the outside, nothing seems to have changed. Your workstation is the same, your activities at work haven't changed, and your coworkers haven't changed. There is no Grand Opening ceremony, there is no applause, and no party thrown in your honor from a team of well-wishers. The celebration is happening within you. You know how hard you have worked to stay consistent with all your goals and accelerators.

You have met a sizable challenge in your personal and professional growth by taking the time to sharpen your awareness, harness hidden gems, and stay consistent with your growth accelerators for two months straight. You have adopted daily practices that will endure the test of time if you choose to keep them alive. Everything you have acquired up until this time will give you the confidence, courage, and resilience to navigate roadblocks and setbacks that come at you in your professional growth journey.

Let's take an inventory:

- You recovered your power by getting curious, building your courage muscle, and growing your confidence.

- You stepped out of your comfort zone intentionally many times.

- You chose to co-create your future and did not let life happen to you.

- You worked on the right priorities.

- You have become more intentional about your day and the activities that fill your day.

- You embraced the power of habit and consistency.

- You made the right choices. Choices that aligned with your priorities.

- You centered yourself and worked on a positive mindset every morning.

- You raised your self-awareness by paying attention to your triggers, your emotions, and the reactions of others.

- You improved the quality of your connections at work, making them genuine and less transactional.

- You practiced behaviors you attributed to your future self by staying aligned with your values and showing up as a confident and optimistic professional.

- You are clear about your goals from chapter 5 and are working every day toward them with intention.

You should be feeling more alive and whole now than when you first started. Isn't that reason enough to celebrate? A truly amazing feat in a short span of time.

On launch day, schedule future check-ins with yourself on your calendar. Counting forward from launch day, **pencil in one at four months, six months, nine months, and one year.**

IMPORTANT: If you haven't read the earlier chapters in this book recently, take time to reread them before you proceed. During the launch phase (month one) and post-launch phase (months two through twelve), continue with your acquired best practices. Here's a review of them:

- Stay consistent with your morning routine and your best practices.

- Manage your fears and doubts when they surface with strategies from chapter 4.

- Manage your time with strategies from chapter 4.

- Be sure to stay intentional in every interaction and communication.

- Be present and curious to strengthen your self-awareness and social awareness.

- Continue to record your progress and then reward yourself for consistent actions.

The activities, habits, and practices you acquired to ignite your power are the fuel to propel the design of your future self. Continue to use them every day because consistent execution will give you a sense of control and accomplishment, and, more importantly, it will brighten your days as you build your path to career success.

A Word of Caution

While the objective of this book is to get you to your goal and help you enjoy the fruits of your labor, it is not about working harder and doing more. It's not about doubling down. Feeling stressed and overwhelmed as you push yourself forward is a recipe for disaster. The tools of the S.H.I.F.T. framework I have shared so far will help you slow down to focus on what is truly important to sustain your growth for years to come. It's mostly *inner work* within one or two of your career focused areas. If your workdays tend to be full, attempt no more than one career-focused goal at a time. Your self-awareness and social awareness will plummet if you end up adopting a frenetic pace at work. Reflection and acute observation skills are only possible with a calm frame of mind. With that said, are you ready to build up your arsenal of tools and techniques to forge your path to fulfillment?

Review your personal definition of success. Check in with yourself and see if your definition of success needs to be refined with the gems you have recently uncovered. Remember, this is the step where you get to define your unique value proposition. In other words, *you* get to decide on your **brand**.

When you look holistically at your life and consider all the important domains—home, health, work, relationships, fun, and play—you can determine your available capacity at this point in your life. Based on your current situation, you choose how hard you want to push your **brand** at work. The boundaries you determine should work well with your other priorities in life. You might choose to operate in a highly specialized role with relatively low responsibility or you may want to go all in and drive toward an executive role with broader and larger responsibilities. It's up to you.

Brands that endure in the marketplace typically solve a problem, are easy and reliable to use, and receive the highest customer ratings. Similarly, the brand you build must be that of a problem solver (you get to define the problem you solve) and showcase your core competencies. This includes how you show up every day at work. Your brand should lead your team members and supervisors to conclude that you are competent, effective, helpful, easy to work with, and reliable.

In the prior chapters, you were diligently building the foundation for this step by working on best practices for building a positive mindset, staying consistent, intentional, self-aware, and socially aware and managing your time, fears, and emotions—all under the purview of self-efficacy, self-regulation, and people skills.

Now take a look at some best practices to elevate your **brand profile at work.** While doing their job of raising your brand visibility, the suggested best practices in this section will also help you overcome obstacles and do what is commonly referred to as "sharpening your saw."

This work does not have a defined end date. You set the pace. This section builds on the effort and results from your earlier work to amplify your impact in the workplace. The best practices here will lead you to a way of working that accelerates your career progress and gives you more control over its direction. With regular practice, you will feel whole and in command of your agenda. You have empowered yourself by following the steps in this framework and now you will be co-creating a professional brand that fits well within your current role and then beyond to future roles.

During this phase, continue to make progress on the goals you set earlier. For example, receiving mastery certifications, becoming an effective communicator, earning the respect of your direct reports, or perhaps even successfully negotiating a salary increase. Continuing this work is essential and, as an added benefit, completing the one-year time-boxed goal from the previous chapter will boost your motivation to carry on.

You started this process because of your disillusionment with the status quo. You knew you deserved better. You have uncovered reasons to take ownership of your journey toward fulfillment. Your success to date in this journey is largely attributable to the discipline you have shown in your daily actions and practices. This is the perfect time to share this powerful quote:

> *We must all suffer from one of two pains: the pain of discipline or the pain of regret. The difference is discipline weighs ounces while regret weighs tons.* — **Jim Rohn**

You are in a much better place today because you chose the pain of discipline now rather than suffer the much heavier pain of regret later.

Be the Change You Want to See

Your presence, your aura, and your actions can inspire and influence others to act. Recall your efforts in discovering your personal power from the last chapter. The way you show up directly impacts the experience of your peers and your leaders. The changes you make can inspire them to change their attitude toward you and inspire them to mirror your actions. You become the catalyst for change. As Mahatma Gandhi said, "Be the change you want to see."

If you feel no one listens, really listens, to ideas and suggestions shared by your coworkers and colleagues, there is something you can do to start building your brand. You can initiate engagement by asking thoughtful follow-up questions after a suggestion is offered. That very act of active listening with meaningful follow-ups gives out the "I am a leader" vibe. Have you noticed others pretending to listen by nodding their heads? Often, it is just an act to look attentive. The questions you ask will validate your coworkers, and your empathy and thoughtfulness will slowly win you a tribe of well-wishers. With that, your sphere of influence will expand to previously unattained levels.

When you believe you are a leader, you will communicate like a leader. Soon you will start noticing team members using your words or phrase choice in an email or in a meeting. People will reach out to you to get your opinion. Your influence will permeate across your team and even beyond.

Be Adaptable

Adaptability is one of those traits that is always in high demand. It is a mindset that must be intentionally developed and regularly nurtured. Be willing to adjust your plans in response to shifting priorities, new processes, new technology, new leadership, and new responsibilities. To demonstrate your adaptability, learn to flex when your preferred option is unavailable. Leaders will view you as an ideal employee and team player if you can accept alternative ideas and remain unflappable when an unexpected change occurs.

Once I spent a few months creating a value proposition proposal to raise my visibility and brand for a specific executive and even scheduled a meeting five weeks out to present it. Two days before the meeting, there was an organization-wide announcement that this leader was leaving the company. My hard work preparing for the meeting seemed like a complete waste of time at that moment. I admit I let myself wallow in self-pity for a couple of days. I had a choice to make: stay bitter or adapt, and adapt I did. I went back to the drawing board and devised an altogether new plan that later proved to be a gift from above. That original setback turned out to be a boon to my career.

Given the changing business environment, be ready to quickly switch and adjust plans. Others may whine or complain about the "change," but you will ask deeper questions about what is behind the change and determine how you can help accommodate it. Change is inevitable; how you handle it is up to you. Adaptability allows you to approach challenges resulting from change with a positive mindset and participate in coming up with an optimal solution—problem-solving, another invaluable skill set for your career progress.

A.M.P. Up Your Game

You are on your way to becoming a valued brand at work. You have identified your core competency and soft skills. You have remedied traits and habits that were obstacles. You have developed new career-promoting habits. Because you worked on your goals consistently, others naturally conclude that you are competent, effective, helpful, easy to work with, and always reliable. The next step is to elevate your brand.

Application of the A.M.P. strategy will enhance your sense of purpose and commitment. It will pump up the quality of your workday and ensure that you are aligning your actions to the overall objective of your brand. A.M.P. stands for Autonomy, Mastery, and Purpose. Daniel Pink's *Drive: The Surprising Truth About What Motivates Us* proved that these are the primary intrinsic motivators. I am recontextualizing these as areas that help nurture and accentuate your brand.

A is for Autonomy

Autonomy is the freedom to act without permission. You may feel you have no power to initiate changes at work given your title or job description. You may not have a C-suite role, but you have more freedom in your role than you assume. Organizations have woken up to employee grievances after the recent Great Resignation movement. Lack of flexibility and autonomy underpinned some of the primary concerns. The hotel chain Four Seasons delivers some of the best services in the world. Their employees are told to do whatever they think is right when servicing the customer. That level of trust and respect placed with the frontline workers explains the great customer service.

You may be shaking your head at this point to claim that you have no freedom to act autonomously in your current role. To which I can confidently say, you have more freedom to act than you are ready to acknowledge. Don't let your job description hold you back. Look for ways to craft a role that blends old with some new value-add. Look for opportunities to make a difference. It starts with being proactive. This is the significant ability to see problems before they happen and offer solutions.

With your heightened curiosity and focus on self-awareness and social awareness these last several weeks, you may start noticing areas for improvement in your department or you may see an opportunity to bridge an operational gap between two partnering functional teams. You might offer to lead the implementation of a solution you suggest in a meeting with your boss. Don't make your solution additional work for anyone else. Being proactive is taking charge and making things happen instead of waiting for someone else to do it. When you take initiative by helping, by stepping up, by seeing an issue and offering a solution, you will be noticed and your exposure will grow. Here are a few ideas to ponder:

- Can you break up non-productive silos at work?

- Is there a way to build a bridge to a functional area that regularly misses opportunities to communicate a change?

- Is there a service or skill you can offer to others on your team?

- Do you have a hobby or interest that you can bring out of the shadows and create engagement in that area with your peers—like starting a weekly book club that meets during lunch? A friend of mine noticed an opportunity and took the initiative to start an Affinity Group program in her company. If you are unfamiliar with this term, an Affinity Group in an organization is a group of employees linked by a common purpose and interest. These groups play a vital role in ensuring an inclusive environment where everyone feels valued, included, and empowered to succeed. Setting up such a group was a lot of work for my friend, but it got her much-needed visibility and set her up for a promotion into leadership.

M for Mastery

In almost all theories related to motivation, mastery is a constant. It's a push from within us to perfect a task or skill. One of my mentees was recognized as the go-to person for process improvement in her department. She earned that reputation because she helped eliminate redundancies in certain time-consuming processes. She was recognized as a master of process improvement. That became a significant part of her brand.

One of my coaching clients was looking for suggestions for greater visibility at work. He was good with spreadsheets, so I encouraged him to master everything in Excel and use that skill to build his visibility. Soon he was offering his analysis and reporting services to those who needed them in his department. Before long, his boss was offering up his services to other functional areas. That helped both their reputations.

My client's visibility grew, and his mastery was often mentioned in conversations among senior leaders.

Executives of large organizations know that mastery shown in core functional areas leads to better productivity and performance. They are often puzzled by the lack of enthusiasm in their employees to master essential skills even when free courses are made available in their learning and development libraries. Take advantage of mastery opportunities available in your company and stand out as proactive while simultaneously upskilling. Focus on skills that increase your significance and contribution at work. Evaluate your strengths—communication, relationship building, leadership, documentation, problem-solving, decision-making—and enhance them as part of your new brand identity.

Mastery could be a key competency of the brand you are trying to cultivate. The journey to mastery will increase your investment and commitment to your current role, increase your value to your company, and make you more visible. A win across the board. Your leaders will appreciate that you are adding value, increasing efficiency and production, communicating effectively, building healthy partnerships—whatever your skill mastery offers. The sense of pride and fulfillment that accompanies mastery will permeate every hour of your workday.

What can you master to help elevate your brand?

P for Purpose

Simon Sinek encourages everyone to "find your 'why.'" When you know your *why*, navigating a challenging road is possible. Sometimes that *why* is elusive; sometimes it is obvious. Sometimes getting there is easy; sometimes it's hard. During certain phases in your career, your *why* is strong; at other times it's weak.

For example, when you know a particular industry certification will get you a promotion and better paycheck, you will work at it. Even if it means getting up at four a.m. to prepare. Your purpose will follow you everywhere during that certification preparation phase, and it will pull you forward.

Endowing your work with purpose answers your *why*. Purpose makes a winning formula for career enthusiasm and progression. Here, the purpose is built, not found. Working with a sense of purpose every day is an act of will. It requires reflection, gratitude, and consistent practice. If your actions and behavior convey a passion, just imagine the shift in perceptions at your job. Your brand will be solidified as helpful, easy to work with, and reliable. Every organization that touts teamwork and collaboration as a core value will embrace that brand. Here are some considerations that may help endow your work with purpose:

1. Whom do you serve? Is it clients of your company, consumers of your product, or staff or departments within your company?

2. Why do you work? Is your reason aligned with your industry's purpose? Is it for your professional success or for the excitement of learning new skills and the accompanying professional growth? Is it for a paycheck to support your family?

3. With whom do you work? Do you enjoy the company of your work colleagues? Do you look forward to conversations and hanging out with them? Do they give you a sense of community? Do you feel like you belong?

4. What does your bright future look like? Are you working today to build a better tomorrow? Does the vision of your future pull you forward?

To illustrate the importance of service or purpose, consider this Yale study conducted by professor Amy Wrzesniewski.[2] This in-depth study of hospital custodial staff was to determine what helped certain members of the custodial team members excel. The study uncovered a practice among the happiest and most effective custodians. These custodial workers focused intensely on serving patients. They practiced "job crafting" whereby they created the work they wanted to do out of the work they'd been assigned to do. For example, one rearranged artwork in rooms to stimulate a comatose patient's brain; others learned about the chemicals used in cleaning supplies to avoid inadvertently irritating patients' conditions.

---

[2] Amy Wrzesniewski. Job crafting and creating meaning in your work. ReWord editors. April 29, 2015. *https://rework.withgoogle.com/blog/job-crafting-and-creating-meaning-in-your-work/.*

They found these extra services meaningful and worthwhile. In essence, they job crafted their work to fulfill their *why*.

If you let autonomy, mastery, and purpose stay on your radar, you will start recognizing opportunities to serve, grow your expertise, and, above all, wake up excited to get to work every day. When you consistently A.M.P. up at work, you will start showing up differently, and your personality will get the added glow of feeling satisfied and fulfilled!

Opportunities and Threats — The L.E.N.S. Solution

Opportunities are everywhere, and threats are never far behind. Transforming yourself and your career path following the S.H.I.F.T. plan does not mean there will never be bumps to overcome.

Weeks and months of effort can suddenly be derailed by an unexpected event or circumstance such as a company reorganization. Or you may hit a brick wall with a boss or a competitor blocking your progress. Political battles and unfair power dynamics are common in organizations, and they may take a toll on you.

It's important to recognize—even plan for—these obstacles, because they will occur. The desired response is to circumvent any threat where possible or, alternatively, figure out a way to regroup, adjust your plan, and identify a new opportunity. The L.E.N.S. solution can help you shift your perspective when you feel stuck. It's the adoption of a mindset that brings opportunities into focus and uncovers clues for navigating challenging situations. Look at the guidance below as insights to apply when confronted with a situation that makes you feel boxed in or when that feeling of "none of this matters" overwhelms you and you want to throw your hands up in the air and say "I'm done."

I have been there. Everything feels pointless. Days start having a déjà vu feeling, the feeling of same old same old. With your new and refreshed vision of your future self, this blah existence should no longer be acceptable to you. When confronted with a threat that muddies your vision, intentionally choose a "**vuja de**" attitude. This is a made-up phrase coined by comedian George Carlin. It's the opposite of déjà vu. Vuja de is the feeling when a familiar routine feels fresh like it never happened before. When you are feeling uninspired or defeated and you need to reach for a fresh positive perspective and fast, use L.E.N.S.: Look and Listen, Examine, Notice Alternatives, Strive for Inventiveness. The following stories and scenarios illustrate common problems and the solutions offered by L.E.N.S.

Look and listen

When your problem is screaming that you are totally stuck, get curious about the situation. Pay attention to everything around you. Look and listen. There are clues everywhere that will help you get unstuck. Sometimes, there is an opportunity hiding in plain sight. Someone may make a casual remark about another person in the hierarchy moving to another team. What could that mean for you? Someone posted an open position on the job board without making any announcement. Do you periodically check the job board? If your company is going through a reorganization, what new skills can you bring to the table? Closer scrutiny of a crisis or a threat can yield a treasure trove of opportunities.

You are familiar with my story of feeling invisible at work. A casual comment made to me was life-changing because I actually listened to it. I was participating in Toastmasters and right after my speech, a work colleague casually suggested that I should do more speaking in my day job. I was a programmer at that time with no real opportunities to present in front of a room. How could I do more speaking? That off-the-cuff suggestion lingered with me. I stayed with it for a while and finally identified the right leader in the hierarchy, with the right decision-making authority, and made a persuasive case for facilitating brainstorming sessions for an upcoming major transformation initiative. I was given the green light with a few stipulations. It was a perfect opportunity to be in the spotlight and showcase my underutilized skills. By paying attention to a casual suggestion, I flipped my "I am invisible" narrative.

Examine

Sometimes a problem feels unsolvable because we may have framed it around incorrect assumptions. This type of scenario will require you to examine your assumptions by asking better questions. Sometimes we box ourselves in with broad generalizations that are a direct outcome of our biases and emotions. For example, when you rush to conclude that your boss is a jerk, you will leave yourself with no options for solutions. That broad generalization will keep you stuck and, more importantly, it will steal your sense of control. If you get stuck with a statement like that, you need to break the problem into chunks where you can actually do something to create change.

How do you do that? First, accept that biases and emotions are in play. Then you determine what is actually going on. You look at the core issue and what surrounding events or actions contributed to your broad generalization. Start writing about the situations that caused you to arrive at that conclusion. You may uncover that your boss is a reasonable person to work with, but he has a blind spot in one or two areas that caused the issue at hand. Those areas that frustrate you may need a separate solution. This approach gets you unstuck as opposed to labeling your boss with a broad brush. Whatever you uncover, now you can direct your attention to how you can plan around it. Here is an undeniable fact: better questions get better answers. Better answers can lead to better decisions and actions. Examine your assumptions and biases.

Notice alternatives

We see every situation through the lens of our biases and filters. Often, people are surprised when they hear that reality is subjective. We know, for instance, two people can witness the same scene and share varying accounts of what happened, what they "saw." People can have the same experience, yet each one will process that experience differently. Two coworkers from the same suburban neighborhood have the same 90-minute commute to work. One is fixated on the wasted time every day, and the other appreciates the privacy it affords her to learn from her favorite podcasts. Who has a more enjoyable day?

When you feel stuck or uninspired, look for silver linings and consider alternatives that could shift your perspective. Take the time to connect your mundane and boring tasks to a higher purpose—like your long-term goals—and they no longer feel like such a drag on your energy and emotions. Use a new frame that assigns meaning and purpose the next time you review your job description or get assigned an unwelcome task. Perspective matters. Notice alternatives to help you get unstuck.

Strive for inventiveness

Your inventiveness holds the key to more enjoyable days at work. When your day includes a repetitive task or a task you do not enjoy, use something like gamification to reframe the task so that you can complete it and move on. Trying to beat the clock on completion time is a gamification approach. A person whose job entailed binding multiple project reports added a slot machine image on the tool, so it wasn't just pulling the hole-punch handle. Pretty creative! Another option is to give yourself a reward even if it is just getting up to get a cup of coffee or tea after you complete a boring and tedious task. Acknowledge that once the task is done, you can concentrate on tasks that you prefer doing. Sometimes, just clearing an unwelcome task from your to-do list is a reward. Every role has activities that can drain your energy. Use your creative energy to fend off feeling drained.

Sometimes you may have to call upon your imagination. When I am not in the mood to fix dinner on weeknights, I pretend I am Nigella Lawson, the famous British chef. My active imagination believes that I have a million subscribers on YouTube. As I assemble the ingredients, I pretend that the camera is on me and I speak with my fake British accent, "A pinch of salt" and "dash of pepper" and voilà—the dish is done. All this may sound silly, but if you can brighten your day, why not challenge the blues by being inventive?

Up until this moment in your execution journey to Launch Day, you had a front-row seat to witness your growth in two short months. You have also developed a deeper understanding of yourself and of those around you. The journey may not have been straight and smooth, but you managed to hold on. You are taking in great quantities of new information and grasping new revelations.

This is a good stopping point in this chapter to reflect. You have learned the techniques to define, build, and enhance your brand. You have techniques to overcome setbacks and boredom. You are continuing to execute on the goals you set originally, and you are observing and paying attention to everything around you. Now, with the recommendations in this chapter, you can proactively seek out opportunities. During regular intervals in your execution journey, you will need time for reflection and introspection to put everything into best practical use. After every two to three weeks, review and respond to the following questions in your notebook as candidly as possible:

1. What proactive activity have you initiated at work that would qualify as you acting with autonomy?

2. What progress have you made to either increase the visibility of your brand at work or fill you with joy?

3. Are you still aligned with a purpose that gives you forward momentum energy?

4. Where have you used the L.E.N.S. perspective-shifting framework to solve a problem at work?

5. Are you becoming a role model for adaptability?

6. When were you being the change you want to see?

Commit to your scheduled periodic check-ins at four, six, nine, and twelve months to look back at where you were when you started and where you are at each check-in period. This will show you how far you have come at each milestone.

Four Months, Six Months, Nine Months, Twelve Months Check-In Assessments

Here are some questions to consider regarding your advancement at work during these check-in milestone assessments.

Write your thoughts and observations in your notebook.

- How do feel about your current situation?

- Are you feeling more seen?

- Are you feeling more valued?

- Are you more appreciated at work?

- Are you feeling well utilized?

- Have you created allies?

- Is there someone in particular you want to make your ally? Why? How will you go about doing this?

- Has any manager, leader, or project team leader in your functional area who previously ignored you paid attention to your suggestions and opinions recently?

- On a scale from 1 to 10 with ten being the highest, where is your job satisfaction?

- Write in your notebook or create a recording describing your current inner world. Include your desires, areas you are still working on, any frustrations, new values, and priority realignments. What are the primary things you are currently working on changing or polishing?

Take some time to retrieve and review your **before snapshot** from the beginning of your journey a few months ago. Compare this information to where you are now. **Write down the specific gains in your notebook.** Remember, both personal and professional development are about incremental gains you have made.

After your review, are you where you planned to be at this stage of your journey? If there are areas that are slow to resolve, do not worry. Reflect on what might be causing the issue. If it is in an area out of your control, think of new ways to influence a change. Have you set too high a bar for too short a time? Are you being too tough on yourself in your qualitative assessment? Have you missed a notable indicator of a gain? Did you receive a compliment or two that was aligned with a goal on your list? Have you maintained your consistency in your morning routine and the steps in your S.H.I.F.T. journey? Do you need to shore up your "why"?

It needs to be recognized that new facts on the ground might necessitate a change in your goals and direction. Think about the lesson of adaptability. Be assured that there are always multiple paths to your ultimate destination. Thoughtful reflection and new lessons learned during your journey will help you recalibrate your progress from a perspective of future identity, self-awareness, and social awareness. The most important indicator that you are operating at or toward your potential is that you feel excited about your future again.

If you feel satisfied with your progress after the four milestone check-ins, you are ready to walk into a future where you have all the experience, wisdom, tools, and techniques to thrive and flourish wherever you choose.

CHAPTER SUMMARY

- **Brands** that endure in the marketplace typically solve a problem, are easy and reliable to use, and differentiate themselves. Building your adaptability muscle and being the change you want to see helps create your unique value proposition—your brand—at work.

- When intrinsic motivators are applied, they will enhance your commitment and your brand and pump up the quality of your workday.

- It is important to plan for obstacles in your growth journey. Use a practical approach to sharpen your observation skills and reframe an issue to navigate your way out of a crisis.

CHAPTER 7

THRIVE AND FLOURISH

Remember the bamboo tree from chapter 5 that shoots up almost 90 feet in a month after almost five years of dormancy? That final push to awe-inspiring heights is what this section is about. This phase is intended to catapult your impact and leave you with a deep sense of fulfillment.

You kicked off PROJECT YOU and delivered on the objectives you laid out in the beginning. You are now the brand that can scale up to become the best version of yourself. Scaling up is like all the iPhone releases that followed the initial launch. You have contributed value, developed and refined your brand, and raised your profile at work. A uniquely differentiated brand is emerging. Now, it is time to look for ways to scale up for a broader reach and impact. Your focused attention on awareness, consistency, and intentionality contributed to your recent gains. Besides that, you now know what is important to you.

You realize now that you are in charge of your career trajectory and overall fulfillment. You have clarity and you have options. You are observing, studying, evaluating, and making decisions on your direction every single day. You are developing an **owner's mindset**. An owner's mindset refers to a way of thinking and approaching tasks as if you are the owner of a business. It means being responsible and accountable for your actions and decisions. Instead of blaming others, an owner takes ownership of their progress. An owner is focused on continuously improving and growing. It is a mindset that values long-term success over short-term gains. This means that important decisions that an owner makes may not provide immediate benefits but are better for growth in the long run.

This mindset will serve you well as you continue your journey, because you have already demonstrated that you have what it takes and now you are going to reach for heights that will help you express your true potential. The pain and agony of unexpressed potential is going to be a thing of the past.

Now aim for the stars and live your potential. The stars are what you choose them to be. It need not be, and should not be, a race against your competitor. For most people, falling into a comparison trap is a debilitating move that keeps you away from your authentic self. Never forget that you are an owner now in charge of your direction. There is no one size fits all timeline. Your scaling-up journey does not have a universal timeline. Remember your life has many key domains (home, family, friends, health, work, fun, and play) that contribute to your fulfillment. Often one or two domains dominate in a particular chapter of life. Keeping all the domains in perfect balance all the time would be too great a challenge, but finding a proper, workable, livable balance for you for right now is a good goal.

Thriving and flourishing is a combination of growth, success, and fulfillment. Until this moment you have been on a growth journey with achievements that hopefully have made you proud. Your sense of self is on a more solid footing now. Seeing how far you have come in such a short period fills you with confidence and a readiness to tackle what's next. Your morning routine with journaling has shifted your mindset to one of optimism. Most therapists and researchers will agree that having a positive perspective and an optimistic mindset are key contributors to that sense of fulfillment.

You have also discovered your personal power through inner work, discipline, adaptability, and staying intentional. You have taken back your power in relationships that you unknowingly gave away during days of insecurity and doubt.

This new, brave persona has enabled you to explore more to expand your reach. Your values, strengths, interests, passion, and purpose were brought into sharper focus. You understand the real you and you have a better understanding of others. Relationships at work are more rewarding. You also know that a meaningful relationship feels different, better, than a purely transactional one. Your can-do attitude and your proactive approach are an inspiration for others. Your very presence empowers others to do better.

The techniques and tools at your disposal now are like a genie that can grant you success for a defined goal. You will have other opportunities at other times in your life to pick new options that let you continue to thrive and flourish.

Let me share a few sample scenarios that lay out possibilities in terms of career direction awaiting you. You may choose an entirely different path, but this sampling below is to showcase possible directions your career may take. You will enjoy architecting your future, and when you are having fun every day designing a brighter future, time will fly.

> *The bad news is time flies. The good news is you're the pilot.* — **Michael Altshuler**

These scenarios are framed as a look back and a look forward. Take some time to reflect on them.

SCENARIO 1
You started off your corporate career as a driven and ambitious professional and then, for a multitude of reasons, you felt blocked and sidelined. Now, with the S.H.I.F.T. approach, you have experienced the early, yet tangible, benefits to reclaim your drive and passion. You are more intentional and consistent and have amended those behaviors and traits that caused you trouble in the past. You have enhanced your communication and active listening skills.

What will you choose as the next step? You are looking at the corporate ladder and have set your sights on where you want to land first. With that end in mind, you start your investigation and utilize your toolkit to advance your agenda. Your now keen observation skills can help you find perfect opportunities to showcase your brand. You can see that new title next to your profile picture on LinkedIn and an awe-inspiring total compensation packet coming your way. You are thriving and flourishing because you are getting to fulfill your potential.

SCENARIO 2
You dreaded Sunday evenings because there was nothing remotely fun or inspiring to look forward to in the work week ahead. On occasion, you even labeled your coming week as toxic. You had a gnawing feeling that your punching-in and punching-out attitude may be to blame. You picked up this book to see if finding fulfillment was possible for someone in your situation. With the help of your self-awareness and social awareness journey over this last year, you are now connecting with others easily and naturally. Your team members drop by casually to chat with you. Your blind spots have been addressed. With better time management, you are able to find time for relaxed conversations with coworkers.

What will you choose as the next step? Maybe you learned that big responsibilities that come with rapid career acceleration are not your cup of tea. Your responsibilities at home are far more critical at this time. Maybe a newly discovered connection with your boss helped you acquire opportunities to explore your unique value proposition. You work toward becoming a subject matter expert, and your expertise is valued by your peers and leaders. Isn't it great living your fullest potential, feeling connected to others, and waking up excited on Monday morning? Maybe you can see yourself thriving and flourishing right where you are.

SCENARIO 3

You were in peak frustration mode when you picked up this book. You were feeling invisible, undervalued, and underutilized. Promotions were passing you by. And it seemed no one cared enough to give you honest feedback. Now, after working with your S.H.I.F.T. plan, your observation, self-awareness, and social awareness sensitivities have peaked. You are picking up all kinds of clues in your environment. You are thrilled to be recognizing these clues because now you know what to address, and you have a plan to do just that.

What will you choose as the next step? This depends on what you discovered and what you chose to concentrate on. You might hire a coach to help refine and guide your leadership persona. You see yourself blossoming as a leader and getting that first promotion followed by others in quick succession. Or you might realize that you are more a technical expert and acquire even greater mastery. You realize you have built a compelling brand that no one can ignore and that makes you smile.

SCENARIO 4

When you picked up this book, you knew that your acceptance of the status quo was not going to serve you well in the future. Others around you were getting ahead, making you question your own complacency. You worried about becoming a statistic in the next company layoff. Complacency may have set in because initiating a change felt too hard or it may have to do with you not being in the right role to begin with.

Then you chose to dive deep into the S.H.I.F.T. approach. You regularly applied the look and listen and examine strategies to discover opportunities available to you right in your organization. You unexpectedly discover that you are very curious about the work produced by xyz team. It seems fun and interesting. After repeated whispers from your intuition nudging you in that direction, you have decided to explore your interests further by scheduling a coffee with a team leader in that department.

What will you choose as the next step? You made new friends in that area and your boss generously gave you the time to explore your interest. You took courses at a college nearby and soon started producing praise-worthy work. In less than a year after the initial contact with the xyz team leader, you were splitting your time 50-50 to help with a staffing shortfall in that team. When the next job opening showed up in that department, you were the first one to raise your hand. You are now convinced that you have uncovered your calling and passion. It is so easy to see yourself thriving and flourishing here. You have kissed your apathy goodbye.

SCENARIO 5
You started exploring the S.H.I.F.T. growth journey because a sense of deep malaise was overpowering you. You were beginning to wonder if your old enthusiastic self ever existed. *How did I get here* was constantly on loop in your head. As

you started applying the strategies shared in the A.M.P. up strategy, especially autonomy and mastery, a certain spark was lit. You have uncovered a skill set to specialize in. The early signs have indicated that there is a demand for that skill in your organization. The feeling of malaise is evaporating.

What will you choose as the next step? You have chosen to stay with the discovery and excel in this new craft. Your passion for it takes you to online courses and industry competitions. Your success in those competitions is prompting your leaders to consider you a flight risk and your pay raises have been generous. The cherry on top is seeing others using your product and gushing over its utility. Suddenly, you have amazing options and opportunities available to you. You feel totally in command of your life and the old enthusiastic personality is back and brimming over.

SCENARIO 6

You picked up this book because you felt you had stagnated in your current leadership role for too long. You wanted to be recognized and valued as a thought leader and executive of the company. As you progressed through this growth program, you noticed meaningful shifts in your mindset and attitude. The morning routine, daily reflection, and setting of intentions helped you get there. With the consistent application of the techniques in "Forge Your Path," you discovered that you loved helping others get unstuck and reach their potential. People are now stopping by your office and thanking you for your help in solving their problems. Your guidance and wisdom are making a measurable impact in your organization, and the results have pleased you more than any other recent achievement.

What will you choose as the next step? Given the impact and reach of this new discovery, you now want to share your latent talent with a broader audience. Perhaps become a mentor to many, conduct group coaching sessions at work, or start your own coaching business in the next few years. Working long hours and navigating the political landmines no longer hold allure for you. Your prior definition of success is no longer in alignment with your values. You realize that sometimes it is about stepping back and doing something different that will help you thrive and flourish.

SCENARIO 7

Getting ahead in your company is important to you and that triggered your close examination of this framework. As you have considered your circumstance, you have picked up on clues that your communication skills were lacking and concluded that it was the singular impediment to career advancement. You decided to dedicate yourself to better communication and conversations every day. You analyzed all the types of communication you engage in throughout the day, verbal and written. You became intentional in every presentation, in every question you asked, and email you wrote. You know you are improving because there are minimal signs of confusion in the audience during the presentation and minimal clarification requests in your inbox.

What will you choose as the next step? You decide to dig deeper into this area because the more you experience the rewards, the more you are enjoying the process of refining and sharpening your communication skills. You consistently think about: Who is in the audience? What kind of information is anticipated? What is the outcome you desire? Is the message clear, concise, and comprehensive? Leaders in your organization marvel at your aptitude. You have received several clues that your promotion is right around the corner. You are bursting at the seams with joy because you architected this amazing turnaround.

The Right Place to Flourish

I bought a gardenia plant for my screened-in porch for the sweet fragrance of the showy white flowers. I cared for the plant diligently, following directions on the label. To my great disappointment, it never bloomed. Instead, leaves began dropping and white cottony stuff developed despite administering recommended treatments. I persisted for four months. There were periods of recovery and then a relapse to the old diseased condition. The plant looked sad and listless. I never saw a single white flower.

Finally, I gave up on my vision of a scented porch and moved my potted gardenia to my backyard with a plan to discard it. After I moved it outdoors, I promptly forgot about it. A few weeks later when I was walking in my backyard, I noticed that my sad gardenia plant had fresh shiny green leaves. On closer inspection, I saw the beginnings of a white bud. I couldn't believe my eyes. After that first flower many more came. My gardenia is a thriving plant now with fragrant blossoms.

What happened? I realized that when I relocated it, I had unintentionally moved it to a perfect spot for early morning sun. That bright spot of sunshine was all that was needed. With the right conditions, any plant can blossom. So, also, can people. The perfect spot of sunlight for you is your self-awareness, your social awareness, and the consistency of working on the "right" tasks. That magic formula will serve as the right condition for the expression of your inner genius and unleashing your potential at work, allowing you to thrive and flourish.

CHAPTER SUMMARY

- With a positive mindset and focused effort, you have started operating with an owner's mindset. You are now in charge of your actions and with that, your career trajectory.

- The consistent use of the best practices you have learned will provide you with the right conditions to allow you to thrive and flourish.

CHAPTER 8

LUCKY YOU

When someone gets a promotion, there are often comments like "They were lucky" or "They are a part of that clique" or "Right place at the right time." In some cases, that might be true. But often it was undercover planning and clever execution on that individual's part that helped achieve the promotion. They prepared for that opportunity. They paid attention, studied the right skills, showcased those skills to the right audience, and exuded confidence and positivity every single day. Unless you are looking closely, that genius execution might be invisible to all except to those with the authority to elevate careers and profiles. Usually, there is more to "luck" than "luck"!

> *Luck is what happens when preparation meets opportunity.* — **Seneca**

> *Chance favors the prepared mind.* — **Louis Pasteur**

Diligence is the mother of good luck. — **Benjamin Franklin**

The step-by-step S.H.I.F.T. framework can make you a LUCKY PERSON, one who exudes positivity and confidence as you execute and deliver meaningful results. As you stay committed to the plan, before long others may claim that *you* are lucky with the opportunities that are coming your way. You, of course, know that you created your own luck. You took steps to S.H.I.F.T.!

- **S**et the stage for success
- **H**arness hidden gems
- **I**gnite your power
- **F**orge your path to fulfillment
- **T**hrive and flourish

Having lived my own S.H.I.F.T. journey, I know this framework can spark meaningful changes in your career and can give you a sense of purpose and accomplishment. This step-by-step approach will guide you to your productive sweet spot by growing your self-awareness and social awareness. What your employer gets is a productive and engaged employee and what employer does not covet that?

An article from July 2022 on the World Economic Forum[3] website shared a comprehensive workforce study by McKinsey & Company covering India, Singapore, United

---

3   Martin Armstrong. Future of Work. Why are Americans quitting their jobs? WeForum.org, July 28, 2022.
    https://www.weforum.org/agenda/2022/07/quitting-jobs-reasons-workplace/

Kingdom, Australia, Canada, and the United States. The top four reasons why employees were quitting their jobs from April 2020 to April 2022 were:

- Lack of career development/advancement
- Inadequate compensation
- Uncaring and uninspiring leaders
- Lack of meaningful work

The pain of the large-scale exodus was felt by the employers, but there was and is a deeper pain felt by unhappy and unfulfilled employees who chose to remain in their roles. They may not have quit like some of their peers, but they experience the same disconnects listed above. In addition, often they must take on an additional workload to cover for their peers who exited the company. Eventually, this leads to burnout and quiet quitting.

As you began reading the earlier chapters of this book, you may have been surprised to learn that *you* could strategically and tactfully address your lack of career advancement and meaningful work. You learned you can do this by regaining your power and using it to influence the outcomes of your choosing. It will take time, but it will happen because the application of these steps is easy and practical. After the initial weeks of habit formation, this process will feel like second nature to you. It will take no additional time on your schedule after the initial short period upfront. With the application of your highly acute awareness traits, you can influence change. If you've done the work, you are seeing that now—lucky you.

I am a living breathing example of this, and so are the ones I coached and influenced. The team to airlift me out of my misery and malaise never showed up. I had to patiently and diligently build my plane and lift off on my own terms. Now you are using your own power to forge ahead to claim your own fulfillment.

It was a strong desire to get unstuck that got you to act on this framework and make it your own. By staying focused and consistent for over a year, you are now experiencing the benefits. The pleasure and satisfaction you now feel are going to sustain your good habits and practices. You understand how the system works and can more or less accurately predict the outcomes of your actions. To a growth-mindset person, a lucky person is someone who experiences positive outcomes because they have the right attitude, work smart, and build a supportive network to eventually land in the right place at the right time. The expectation of success is not left to chance. You know it's all about the right action at the right time.

You have what it takes to make a significant impact in your field. My personal wish for you is to experience the thrilling sensation of fully realizing and living up to your potential, finding opportunities to showcase your talents, and feeling the joy of being a victorious lucky you.

A Recommended Self-Help/Personal Development Reading List

(in no particular order)

Robert Greene, *Mastery*
Rosamund Stone Zander and Benjamin Zander, *The Art of Possibility*
Brené Brown, *Daring Greatly*
Peter F. Drucker, *The Effective Executive*
Timothy Ferriss, *The 4-Hour Workweek*
Bill Burnett and Dave Evans, *Designing Your Work Life*
Robert Greene, *The Laws of Human Nature*
John C. Maxwell, *The 15 Invaluable Laws of Growth*
Mel Robbins, *Take Control of Your Life*
James Clear, *Atomic Habits*
Robert Greene, *48 Laws of Power*
Daniel Kahneman, *Thinking, Fast and Slow*
Martha Beck, *Way of Integrity*
Gary John Bishop, *Unfu*k Yourself*
Andrew S. Grove, *High Output Management*
Ed Catmul and Amy Wallace, *Creativity, Inc.*
Malcom Gladwell, *Talking to Strangers*
Ben Horowitz, *The Hard Thing About Hard Things*
Viktor E. Frankl, *Man's Search for Meaning*
Jocko Willink, *Leadership Strategy and Tactics*
Robin Sharma, *The Everyday Hero Manifesto*
Brené Brown, *Atlas of the Heart*
Chip Conley, *Emotional Equations*

APPENDIX

Personal Values Assessment

Vidya

Prepared by Barrett Values Centre
Date: October 23, 2020

Barrett Values Centre's vision is to create a values driven society. This free assessment will help you become more aware of your own values and how these values influence your decisions and actions.

BARRETT VALUES CENTRE

www.valuescentre.com

Personal Values and Awareness

Our values reflect what is important to us. They are a shorthand way of describing our individual motivations. Together with our beliefs, they are the causal factors that drive our decision-making.

Barrett Seven Levels of Consciousness Model

Values can be positive or fear-based (limiting). For example, honesty, trust and accountability are positive values, whereas blame, revenge and manipulation are potentially limiting, or fear-based, values.

Personal mastery involves overcoming or eliminating our fear-based beliefs. When our beliefs or behaviors are out of alignment with what is really important to us - our values, we lack authenticity.

Every human being on the planet grows and develops within seven well defined areas. These areas are defined in the Barrett Seven Levels of Consciousness Model. Each area focuses on a particular need that is common to all people. The level of growth and development of an individual depends on their ability to satisfy these needs.

At different times you may find that you focus more on some levels and less on others, in response to changing life conditions. It is important to understand that in terms of the seven areas higher is not better; for example it will be difficult for you to focus on helping others if you are having health and money problems.

The seven areas in the development and growth of personal awareness are summarised in this diagram and are described in more detail on page 3.

7 Service
Selfless service

6 Making a Difference
Making a positive difference in the world

5 Internal Cohesion
Finding meaning in existence

4 Transformation
Letting go of fears.
The courage to develop and grow

3 Self Esteem
Feeling a sense of self-worth
Fear: I am not enough

2 Relationship
Feeling protected and loved
Fear: I am not loved enough

1 Survival
Satisfying our physical and survival needs
Fear: I do not have enough

www.valuescentre.com

BARRETT VALUES CENTRE and SEVEN LEVELS OF CONSCIOUSNESS are registered trademarks of Barrett Values Centre, LLC.

Personal Values and Awareness

Common Good

Transformation

Self Interest

Self Interest
The first three areas of awareness – Survival, Relationship and Self-Esteem, focus on our personal self-interest – satisfying our need for security and safety, our need for love and belonging, and our need to feel good about ourselves through the development of a sense of pride in who we are. We feel no sense of lasting satisfaction from being able to meet these needs, but we feel a sense of anxiety if these needs are not met.

Transformation
The focus of the fourth area of awareness, Transformation, is on letting go of fears. During this stage in our development, we establish a sense of our own personal authority, and our own voice. Within the area of Transformation, we choose to live by the values and beliefs that resonate deeply with who we are.

Common Good
The upper three areas of awareness – Internal Cohesion, Making a Difference and Service – focus on our need to find meaning and purpose in our lives. We express that meaning by striving to make our world a better place and by leading a life of selfless service. When these needs are fulfilled they engender deeper levels of motivation and commitment. Within these areas, we learn how to develop an inner compass that guides us into making life affirming decisions.

Personal Mastery
Individuals who focus exclusively on the personal self-interest areas may be influenced by the fears they hold about satisfying their individual needs. They look for approval or reassurance from others.

Individuals who focus exclusively on the satisfaction of the upper common good needs may lack the skills necessary to remain grounded. They can be ineffectual and impractical when it comes to taking care of their basic needs. The most successful individuals are those who balance all of the areas. They are trusting of others, are able to manage complexity, and can respond or adapt to all situations.

In reality people do not operate from any one single area of awareness. They tend to be clustered around three or four areas. Individuals are usually focused at areas 1 through 5, typically with a specific emphasis on Internal Cohesion, the fifth area, in which we seek meaning in our lives.

Your Results
On the next page we will show you how the values you chose map against these seven areas. Positive values will be identified with a blue dot and potentially limiting or fear based values will be shown as a white dot.

www.valuescentre.com

Vidya - Results

From the values you selected it is clear that you are starting to really live your sense of purpose and are cooperating with others for mutual benefit and fulfillment.

Your values show:

- Sharing the lessons of your experience to take charge and guide others is a focus for you.
- Strong moral standards and being true to yourself and your principles shape your decisions and how you live your life.
- In your pursuits, you always strive to be at the top of your game.
- Seeking new opportunities to develop and grow keeps you consistently challenged.
- You appreciate high standards of quality and are driven to maintain these in all aspects of your life.
- You are receptive to others' contributions and demonstrate transparency through your actions and words.
- It is important for you to have meaning and a sense of contentment in your life.
- You like to feel appreciated and acknowledged for your efforts.

The type of values you selected indicates that your individual capabilities are most important to you.

Understanding our values helps us better understand ourselves and why we may act or react in the way that we do. For example, if someone undermines one of your values it can result in feelings of hurt; you would be likely to feel upset if your value of "coaching/ mentoring" was not being honored by someone else. Similarly, if you make a decision which goes against one of your values this may lead you to feel uneasy or unsettled about the decision, because you are not being true to yourself.

7: Selfless service

6: Making a positive difference in the world

5: Finding meaning in existence

4: Letting go of fears.
The courage to develop and grow

3: Feeling a sense of self worth

2: Feeling protected and loved

1: Satisfying our physical and survival needs

Positive: ●   Potentially Limiting (L): ○

	Area
being the best	3
coaching/ mentoring	6
continuous learning	4
ethics	7
excellence	3
integrity	5
leadership	6
openness	5
personal fulfillment	6
recognition	2

www.valuescentre.com

BARRETT VALUES CENTRE and SEVEN LEVELS OF CONSCIOUSNESS are registered trademarks of Barrett Values Centre, LLC.

Thoughts shared from Vidya's audiences . . .

"Vidya was one of the shining stars of the entire Conference. She was 100% professional. She came prepared. And she delivered in spades. Wow! Everyone was moved by Vidya's speech; they were inspired, they learned a lot. She gave them a skill set that will last them a lifetime. I will recommend Vidya Raman every opportunity I get. I look forward to Vidya coming to Dubai to speak." — **Paddy Kennedy, Speaker Chair for the World Women Organization's Global Leadership Conference**

"I enjoyed the personal stories and jokes. Vidya did a great job making it personal. As a speaker, Vidya was captivating. She really kept everyone's attention with her stories. Great job getting everyone involved." — **Hannah Chillag, Lazarus Design Team - conference attendee**

"I enjoyed the fact that Vidya incorporated the tips and tools in her everyday life. She is very engaging as a speaker, and I liked her interaction with the audience." — **Jan Coggin, HStretch - conference attendee**

"I enjoyed the emphasis on the importance of positivity in life and at work. Vidya has great energy as a speaker and a person. You come away with the impression that she truly believes and practices what she teaches. " — **Matt Melcher, Sherrill Furniture - conference attendee**

"Thank you so much for facilitating such an amazing conversation at our chapter Roundtable event! Your background and experience provide an informed perspective on leadership that is both empowering and inspiring. It was clear by the participation level and reactions that you effectively engaged the audience throughout the presentation and delivered on a timely topic! Well done and thanks again!" — **Jason Dwyer, PMI Denver Roundtable event organizer**

"I enjoyed how interactive the speaker was and her sharing of great motivational tips. It was a wonderful presentation. Vidya is very personable and engaging, and she seems to care about every person and the situations we go through." — **M.W, Bassett Furniture**

"I enjoyed learning personal development strategies. Learning that it's a choice to be happy or not. That it is up to me where my future goes. Vidya is a very great speaker. I enjoyed it a lot." — **Elaine Reece, FMCA**

"Constructive from the very beginning, useful information grounded in research and best practices. Engaging speaker. Great resourcing of information." — **Lane Brown, Senior Director, Winston-Salem, NC**

"Vidya was excellent! As the organizer of the event, I received immediate positive feedback from the attendees. The presentation aligned well with our company's core values. I am getting a lot of requests for the recorded video from those who could NOT attend the session." — **LaTanya Holt, Senior Information Security Professional, ATD-US**

"It was a great presentation and Vidya exuded positive energy throughout her entire presentation. She delivered value and shared unique perspectives like seeing the world through 'Vuje De' eyes." — **Soo Lee, Senior PAM Engineer, ATD-US**

"Engaging conversation, high energy with practical examples. Fantastic presenter, very encouraging, speaks from the heart." — **Chinwe Onyeagusi, Queensboro**

"Vidya not only provides tremendous information when she speaks, she packages it with an emotional punch to ensure her audience receives and retains the message she's there to share." — **Rich Hopkins, Denver, CO**

"Vidya is an excellent presenter. I took many notes to help me as I work on my vision for 'who do I want to be' in my life. Fantastic presentation! Very energetic and extremely easy to follow all of the ideas presented. Thank you so much!" — **Maureen Barcinski, Austin, TX**

"The framework was POWERFUL. Great topic – simple and to the point. Examples from real life. Passion and energy—well-reflected." — **Shankar Chandramohan, Director, Austin, TX**

"I enjoyed that the Speaker spoke right to the points, applied the 3 points of public speaking to e-mail crafting and composition. Great body language." — **Arsène Boundaon, Relationship Building presentation**

"Vidya is a very clear, animated speaker, making the presentation all about what we can learn and not all about 'look at what I can accomplish'." — **Marianne Kaufman, Director, DTCC**

"The presentation was very impressive, and Vidya was a comfortable and confident public speaker which made the audience comfortable and interested." — **Jeremy Thomas, San Antonio, TX**

"The importance of journaling and daily consistent habits resonated with me." — **Mike McClamroch, Queensboro**

"I enjoyed the examples and stories. Interesting speaker and I stayed engaged throughout." — **Darren Chamberlain, Queensboro**

"I enjoyed the breakdown of the material and how to reflect on yourself. Excellent speaker, shows passion about the subject." — **Stafford Cathell, NC**

ABOUT THE AUTHOR

Vidya Raman is a motivational speaker and a Maxwell Leadership certified coach. She is passionate about people, communication, and leadership and has over 25 years of experience working in Financial Services in various capacities from programmer to senior leadership. Until she discovered her personal power, she was in an epic struggle for relevance in the corporate world. She spent the last decade of her corporate career as a senior leader and officer in Fortune 500 companies.

A career with its fair share of challenges and struggles has armed Vidya with tools and techniques as well as the experience and insights to cultivate a teachable strategy that she uses to inspire, empower, and educate individuals and audiences to live up to their potential. Her mission is to help corporate employees develop an owner's mindset to scale new heights in success and satisfaction.

Vidya offers keynotes and workshops to her corporate clients and to professional organizations across the country. Her topics cover personal growth strategies, relationship building, leadership skills, women empowerment, and finding joy and meaning at work. She has shared her S.H.I.F.T. framework with a broad range of audiences whose testimonials speak to the value and impact of this approach.

Vidya is an empty nester these days and loves traveling with her husband of 34 years. Walking in her neighborhood in Charlotte, North Carolina, with a good book in her ear and socializing with friends are among her favorite pastimes.

For more information about or to connect with Vidya, visit:
https://vidyaraman.com
https://www.linkedin.com/in/vidyaraman/

www.ingramcontent.com/pod-product-compliance
Lightning Source LLC
Chambersburg PA
CBHW070454100426
42743CB00010B/1618